The
Gentle Giant
and the Beauty Queen

AND THEIR CITY OF STEUBENVILLE, OHIO

MJ Michael

THEY BEAT ALL ODDS!! THIS STORY WILL KICK YOU IN THE
PANTS IF YOU THINK YOU'RE HAVING A BAD DAY!

WestBow
PRESS
A DIVISION OF THOMAS NELSON

WestBow Press books may be ordered through booksellers or by contacting:

WestBow Press
A Division of Thomas Nelson
1663 Liberty Drive
Bloomington, IN 47403
www.westbowpress.com
1-(866) 928-1240

ISBN: 978-1-4497-3516-6 (sc)

Library of Congress Control Number: 2011963341

Printed in the United States of America

WestBow Press rev. date: 12/28/2011

Endorsements

"As a special education teacher, parent mentor and sister of "The Gentle Giant," I think all readers, and especially parents of children with special needs will appreciate the joy and hope that this book shares."
Kathy Kelps Pavlik

"Once in a while a book captures the essence of a place, and this book does so beautifully. Far beyond mere history and culture – it captures the soul of a remarkable place, and a truly remarkable couple. Any excuses you allow yourself in facing your own challenges will disappear as you read this profound true story. Movies are born from stories like this!"
Jim Schmidt, Producer – 'Trade of Innocents'

"M.J. Michael has effectively and lovingly told a story that needed to be told. Your heart will jump with inspiration at this wonderful story of belief and courage. Your obstacles will shrink in size as you follow two people who overcome more odds than most people face in a lifetime."
Ron Ball, Author of several best selling books, Prestonburg, KY

"MJ Michael's true and touching story about a Gentle Giant named David, and his Beauty Queen, Ruthy, takes place in Americana at its best, Steubenville, Ohio. The story and the eastern Ohio town go hand-in-hand. An old friend of mine visited the area with me a few years back. I remember asking him what he thought about my home town. His answer described it best, he said, "These are real people." It may sound a bit trite, but the truth is, yes these are real people with a real life story, a story worth telling and by all means a story worth reading."
Dr. Tony Foglio, Founding Pastor and Pastor Emeritus, Sonrise Community Church San Diego, CA; Author of the Sonrise Devotional Bible and The Discover The Bible; Chairman of the advisory board, World Help, Forest, Va.; Chairman of the board, Primary Focus, Knoxville, TN

"A touching story about two unique individuals who overcame immense obstacles to build lives of faithful love."
Chris Sparks, MA Theology, 2011, Franciscan University of Steubenville

This endearing story illuminates our national responsibility to continue to fight for developmentally disabled funding for those who truly need Governmental assistance. *Congressman Bob McEwen*

"This book is written in such a manner that it inspires you, uplifts you, makes you believe that man CAN rise above and accomplish, even in the face of cruelty, apathy, punishment and obscurity. Yet, at the same time it convicts YOU to be better, be part of the solution, and NOT part of the problem, rising to a higher plain of human existence. The pathos of the Steubenville couple, the heartache, poverty of spirit and upbringing, and then ultimate triumph, salted with poignant anecdotes makes you laugh, sob, sing and ultimately REJOICE! Ms. Michael is obviously passionate, not only about relating to you, the reader, the story of Ruthie and David, but also about conjuring up SUPERB and SPLENDID images of the history of her beloved hometown in Ohio. A family tree, a saga that is well written and humorous so you even laugh out loud at points, leads me to believe this is NOT only a casual must-have read, but has all the cornerstones of a fabulous Hollywood Screenplay opportunity, along the lines of SAM, and Benny and JOON. Please read, enjoy, and celebrate life and the best aspects of LOVE, tenderness, compassion, and caring. Long live hand-holding walks together!"
Dr. Jeff Morrison, Bethesda, MD

As a family counselor of some 40 years I read the book with great enthusiasm and relief to find out that most families don't require drugs nor all the give aways, in order to live normal and happy lives. This tender story proves beyond a shadow of a doubt, that a family that shares their faith, and relies on love is the healthiest family on earth.
Dr. George Bryniawsky Doctorate in Counseling and Training & Development from University of Massachusetts

Acknowledgements

In preparation for this book, there were many who had done work before me on issues of Developmental Disability Independence, the Atmosphere and Culture of the hard working class people in the Steel Mill City of Steubenville and also the History and World Impact of the Franciscan University of Steubenville. I was very fortunate to have the works of the books listed in the Bibliography to enhance the heart warming story of David Kelps and Ruthy Rodgers. I thank those dedicated authors.

Of course the book wouldn't even have been written without the determination and overcoming of our stars, Davey and Ruthy. Their lives provided the substance for many needed life lessons.

I'm very appreciative of the cooperation by both the family of Ruth Ellen Rodgers and the family of David Kelps. Their stories relayed in this book gave us a chance to learn a lot, not only about the developmentally disabled, but the human will of overcoming individuals.

To all of the siblings, nieces, nephews, cousins, aunts and uncles who shared their stories and pictures, a very grateful thank you. A special thanks to my sister-in-law, Kate Reed, who successfully researched Ruthy's *lost years*.

There is one individual family member that has become a very good friend and an irreplaceable source of information about her cousin, Ruth Ellen, and her family background. The case worker was unaware that Ruth even had a family. Therefore, cousin Penny's willingness to meet with me many times and share (even sometimes painful memories) provided another avenue for helping people through the writing of the book. Penny, is precious, giving and has now been reconnected to her cousin through the writing of 'The Gentle Giant and the Beauty Queen'.

The organization, JeffCo Inc, is to be commended for cooperating with the writing of this book, and for providing the care and devotion for Davey, Ruthy and all the others they serve. It has won my accolades for a good job well done. A special thanks to Mike and Brenda, David and Ruth Ellen's case workers, respectively. You were a great help.

While visiting Steubenville during my research, it was a real pleasure to be granted the gracious hospitality of Judge Dan and Connie Spahn. They are dear friends and (in my mind) pillars of the striving and surviving members of the community. Thanks for your time, great bed, gardenia flowers and wonderful breakfasts. It was fun being together. Thank you.

A special thank you to Father Mike, the previous Chancellor of the Franciscan University of Steubenville for taking his precious time to meet with my husband and me about this story.

The Al and Kathy Pavlik family need to be acknowledged and thanked not only for their willingness to share and give towards this book but also for making the successful independent life possible for David and Ruth Ellen to share for 30 years together. Their watchful eye, acceptance and time allotted to assure all was provided for them, was necessary for Dave and Ruth to enjoy sheltered independence.

David and Ruth's lives were better because of all the Kelps siblings' inclusive nature towards two people they loved, who were just *different*.

A special thanks also goes to my author friend, Jerry Hartley, who traveled with me to Steubenville to do a taped interview with David and Ruth Ellen. She contributed many good observations. Thanks, Jerry.

Thanks to Carmen DeStephano for opening the door to me at the United Steel Workers of America local union to gather steel mill history.

No one deserves more thanks for the patience it took during the writing of this book, than my husband, Scott. Never has there been a more supportive husband, than my Scott. He's probably very glad that it's concluded so that he'll no longer hear, "Just a minute" "Can it wait?" "Not today." "I'm hiding away upstairs for a few days." "Could you do it for (or without) me." "I need to go away for a few days!" He has been wonderful as usual! I can't thank him enough for letting me have the time needed to develop this story.

There will be others who deserve much thanks, like my wonderful secretary, Michelle, who has typed and retyped my book and encouraged me to press on. Also thanks needs to be given to those in the publishing and film community who have seen this project even bigger than I did at first.

I appreciate everyone's combined efforts to help many other Davids and Ruth Ellens to live happy, successful independent lives.

Dedication

The dedication of this book is to the wonderful mother, mother-in-law, grandmother, neighborhood mother, and my special Aunt Dorothy Kelps. Aunt Dorothy was a tireless worker, never complained, never spoke ill of anyone, endured hardships with apparent ease, and loved unconditionally. Her life was self-less service to others. I cried at her funeral! She loved us all!

Table of Contents

Preface

The following story that I'm going to share is true. It illuminates the impossible that can become possible when there is:

- A loving and accepting family

- Mother's and Grandmother's prayers

- Strong presence of the Judeo Christian work ethic

- Attitudes of Victory vs. Victimhood

This is a story of love and the tragedy of others that made for this Developmentally Disabled couple's independence. You'll observe contrasting family attitudes and the unbelievable circumstances in others' lives that are beyond comprehension. We'll walk through some lives to celebrate their victories through love and determination.

You'll cheer the contentment, happiness, and love of this special couple. But you'll also be challenged as we see our own evaluations and prejudging of things and people that are *different*. This book makes all of us look at ourselves and question our own tolerance levels in many areas of life.

By the end of this story, most of you living in or visiting Steubenville, Ohio will think a little differently and smile as you see David (7' tall) and Ruthy (5' tall) sauntering down the sidewalk, holding hands as always.

You'll be inspired by secrets of triumph over odds and you'll feel the small victories and blessings that we should celebrate every day.

My hope is that your experience in reading this book will be as enjoyable as the laughs and tears I've experienced as I interviewed and met the remarkable characters that you're about to meet in this true saga.

We may even have to ask, "Do we love enough? Do we have what it takes to make lemonade out of our lemons?"

Introduction

It's my pleasure to introduce you to the primary players in this saga, The Gentle Giant, David, and his Beauty Queen, Ruthy. This part of the book will be just a snap shot of what's to come.

Why the Gentle Giant and Beauty Queen titles? As you walk into their modest home, you'll be immediately impressed with an 8"x10" picture of a truly beautiful blonde child of around four years old. She has beautiful green eyes and the winning smile of a little Beauty Queen. As Ruthy picks up the precious picture from the foyer stand, she'll proudly proclaim that the picture is of herself as the Bethany, West Virginia Little May Queen Winner! It was only a few months later that she contracted the dreaded disease of Spinal Meningitis. Her world changed as the affliction affected her entire left side, leaving her with learning disabilities and a crippled left side that stunted her growth at 5' tall.

Ruthy's Beauty Queen Days[1]

---

1   Compliments of Ruth Ellen Rodgers

Our Gentle Giant David is seven feet tall with size 16 EEEE shoes and weighs 330 lbs. He is a big man. He can be an imposing figure at first glance. You would definitely take a double look to make sure your eyes had truly seen a giant. In fact you could be scared of him endangering you, just by his *hugeness*. Your fears could be magnified if he were to proclaim in his loud guttural voice, "I'm going to 'Hit' you!!" When David tells you he's going to give you information, he loudly states, "I'm going to *hit* you" (with information). Ruthy's case worker informed me that she ducked the first time she heard David say, "I'm going to *hit* you." Much to her relief, David did not hit her but kept talking to *hit* her with information.

David was a large child (only two years older than his brother Ron)[2]

---

2   Compliments of the Kelps Family

To further define David's size, she shared with me that when she needed to take David and Ruthy to an appointment from the workshop, all of them stared at her small car to see how to fold David into the backseat. When she realized that David wasn't going to fit, she resourcefully opened her sun roof and David excitedly and proudly went through town with half of his body extended out of the sun roof opening! Now that had to be a sight! David was a *Happy Camper* on that excursion.

David's size also can be envisioned by the often retold story of David wading out into the lake and proclaiming to his young nieces and nephews, "See, you can come out, it's only up to my waist." Four feet of water! Fortunately they didn't follow.

Shallow Water??[3]

Upon knowing David, all your fears of danger would dissolve. Now he might repeatedly talk your ear off, but he'd never hurt you. At least he'd not hurt you intentionally. In a friendly game of Basketball, he had been assigned to guard my husband, Scott, and keep him from making any baskets. David follows directions very well! Thus, as Scott ascended to put the ball into the hoop, he saw a *Mack Truck* 7 foot 330 lb. David coming with a full body block. Before Scott went crashing down on the pavement, he remembers thinking, "I'm going to die." We all had that immediate thought as we saw Scott fly into the air and crash on concrete! Our son, Scott, went running over to him saying, "Are you ok, are you ok!" almost sure that he wasn't. Thank God that he was. So after that, the Gentle Giant was placed under the basket to just place the balls in the net!

---

3 Compliments of the Kelps Family

Right Before the Knockout[4]

Additionally, I'd forgotten to warn my 5 foot 100 lb blonde housekeeper of David's size and strength. When the whole family came flooding into our home in Fremont, Ohio, amongst the hugs and greetings I looked over to see excited, happy David flinging our Laura into the air with a bear hug! Laura's eyes were huge and wild with freight. I rescued her, and after her heart stopped pounding, introduced her to the family, whom she took care of and loved for many visits.

David is much more a protector than a danger. He so carefully watches over Ruthy's every crippled step. Holding her hand or elbow, he warns her of any possible mishap while they enjoy their walks all over Steubenville. You would never have to even think about being concerned about David's behavior when with Ruthy. With one nudge or glance upward, Ruthy can totally control big David. Its darling to see her correct him should any profanity slip through his lips.

As David's siblings all agree Ruthy is the best thing that ever happened to the Kelps family... As you follow through Ruthy's life you'll be certain that the Kelps family was the best thing that ever happened to Ruthy.

---

4   Compliments of the Kelps Family

Kelps Family Picture with Ruthy[5]

To show you the Giant's gentle side, his family remembers when David was a very big age eight, still conquering his tricycle. He ran over a worm. With concern he jumped off the bike to check on the worm and immediately threw up when he realized that the worm was dead! As gentle as he is, he also has a big heart and loves people. Everyone's his friend. The protection he gives Ruthy is of great value to the shy, scared, abandoned gal he first met.

David's developmental disability from birth was the result of the umbilical cord being wrapped around his neck, thus cutting off oxygen from his brain. Ruthy knew four years with her full mental capacity and strong body, while David struggled with disabilities from the day he was born. But you'll never get Ruthy or David to admit to having any disabilities. Ruthy will argue, "Everyone has a disability, I can do anything that I want."

Both David and Ruthy are so courteous to each other – it's *honey this* or *honey that*. They are kind, honest, friendly, and grateful. The world in their era deemed them both, correctly, mildly retarded due to issues they had no control over, nor could they have prevented. We often forget those facts when we encounter a developmentally disabled person.

---

5   Compliments of the Kelps Family

Like the changes in semantics with *"Bad"* now meaning *"Good,"* the semantics of the developmentally disabled have changed throughout our country's history. Please excuse a word or terminology throughout this book used in explaining disability history. This history includes words that are seen today as demeaning, such as: imbecile, retarded, crippled, feeble minded, and handicapped. These words are used only as they fit the historical context of the time and certainly no insults are intended. The terminology chart listed below reveals much about how society viewed the disabled throughout our history. Today, medical science can make some disabilities invisible.[6]

TERMINOLOGY

- 18th Century
- Cripple
- Insane
- Idiot
- Imbecile
- Lunatic
- Mad
- Deaf and Dumb
- Blind
- Fool
- Simpleton
- Cretin
- Deranged
- Neurotic
- Phobic

- 19th Century
- Cripple
- Deaf and Dumb
- Insane
- Fool
- Idiot

---

6   Floyd, Barbara L. Editor. *From Institutions to Independence.* Published by the University of Toledo Press

- Lunatic
- Mongoloid
- Abnormal
- Cretin
- Epileptic
- Pauper (insane)
- Psychopathic
- Feeble-minded
- Imbecile
- Simpleton

- Early 20th Century
- Backward
- Defective
- Insane
- Dullard
- Fool
- Idiot
- Silent
- Imbecile
- Lunatic
- Mentally retarded
- Mongoloid
- Moron
- Neurotic
- Pauper
- Subnormal
- Cripple
- Feeble-minded
- Mentally ill
- Spastic

- Late 20th Century
- Handicapped
- Emotionally and behaviorally disturbed
- Learning disabled
- PTSD (Post Traumatic Stress Disorder)

- Mentally ill
- Down
- Mentally handicapped
- Mentally retarded
- Polio
- Autistics
- Schizo
- Manic Depressive
- Bi-polar Psychotic

- <u>21st Century</u>
- "Person who is…"
- Partially sighted
- Differently abled
- Mentally ill
- Chronically ill
- Congenitally disabled
- Learning disabled
- Mobility disabled
- Non-vocal, non-verbal
- Developmentally Disabled (DD)[7]

As medicine has prolonged life today, most of us may be in the definition of 'disabled' in our lifetime. The changes in who we define as disabled will undoubtedly impact our future and the understanding of what disabled means and needs. In Toledo there has been an organization for 90 years with many different titles, now called the Ability Center. This is a center for the disabled to gain independent living. It is not an organization seeking charity for their clients, but instead it is a strong advocate pushing the community to support the right of disabled people to live independently.

The Kelps family was never embarrassed of David, due to his size, speech, quirky dress (he had a style unto his own). Never would they treat him with any disrespect. They protected him as the younger brother, even though he was the oldest. One time there was an issue prior to the wedding

---

7   Floyd, Barbara L. Editor. *From Institutions to Independence.* Published by the University of Toledo Press

of one of David's nephews. The bride to be repeatedly asked the family, "What are we going to *do* with David?" When the family had heard this one too many times, David's brother announced, "No matter what you do or how you dress David, he's still going to be retarded and he's still going to be seven feet tall!" For other reasons that wedding never happened.

David's case worker, Mike, reflected for me his first sighting of David and Ruthy sauntering down the street, holding hands. This was long before Mike had entered the field of working with the developmentally disabled. He of course, took a double take to look again and confirm the sight of a huge 7' man walking with a small 5' woman. After reflection, he remembers summarizing, "Guess it's true, there's someone for everyone!" Such is the story of David and Ruthy – the Gentle Giant and the Beauty Queen!

I assure you that when you've finished this book, you'll see in this love story of David and Ruthy and the lives of their family members, the true important qualities of life that make a difference.

Against all odds, these two precious souls at 64 and 66 outlived their doctors' predictions of early childhood deaths. They have been blessed by the providence of God to have found each other and to have enjoyed a wonderful love for 30 years.

As I wrote this book, I kept hearing in my head Tina Turner's song title, "What's love got to do with it?" In this story…EVERYTHING!

Chapter 1
LIMITATIONS???

SSSHHHH….Don't tell David and Ruthy – they won't believe you!

Since this book addresses the independence and happiness of two developmentally disabled individuals, I feel it is important to state their institutional evaluations in the back of this book. I'm certainly not a professional in this field to suggest that all mentally disabled individuals have the capacity to live independently; I'm just the story teller.

It's been brought to my attention that there are major distinctions in levels of mental disabilities. The issues of mental illness are not just disabled, but rather those individuals to whom medication can make it invisible, or a medical doctor and prescription are required for safety for themselves and others.[8]

The Kelps family handled David's disability with diligence and commitment to prepare David for the independent life he lives today. There can be no doubt that the Kelps family truly encompassed Ruthy with their total love and acceptance, saving her from years of loneliness and abandonment. When I asked Ruthy, "Did you like David's mom?" with the biggest of smiles and deeply sincere eyes, she looked at me and softly said, "I loved her."

---

8   Floyd, Barbara L. Editor. *From Institutions to Independence*. Published by University of Toledo Press

Dorothy/Ruth Ellen[9]

When talking to Ruthy about the whole Kelps family, she quickly looked at David and said, "They liked me right away, didn't they?" "Yes, yes they did," responded David. In a way, Ed and Dorothy Kelps prepared both David and Ruthy for their current happiness. This preparation didn't come without much hushed criticism from extended family or church lady opinions. I heard, "I'd have him right by my side, every minute." "I wouldn't let him out of my sight." "Look at the way he takes her head and turns it towards him to tell her something." "I don't know how Dorothy can handle him?" "Do you know they let David visit at Ruthy's place after work?" "I don't know how Dorothy and Ed can be involved in so many things with the responsibility of David." "How naïve they are to encourage the dating of two mentally disabled individuals." and so on.

For sure, Dorothy didn't listen to those opinions, but as her son Ron said, "She just had the insight from God to give David *sheltered independent freedom.* Many times I walked into my aunt's home to see her alone reading her Bible. She was strong and had to be in order to handle a tough steel foreman husband, four other children, and David. And we all loved her!

9   Compliments of the Kelps Family

So what is a disability? Is it physical? Is it a negative perspective of life that keeps us from achieving our potential? Is it a mentally challenged life from birth events or a happening of which one has no control? Well, concerning David and Ruthy, with the Kelps family dedication to them both, you'll see that disabilities are, to a great extent, what we make of them. David and Ruthy don't realize they have disabilities. They've very much succeeded in their world.

America is a country of *Can Do* people; we all love and cheer for the stories of victories over all odds. It brings tears to our eyes as we see a father pushing his physically impaired son in a wheelchair across the finish line at the Special Olympics. Our hearts pound as we see the dedication of a mother slowly moving through a store or an airport with her physically or mentally disabled child. At these sightings we have to check ourselves and our love *quotients* as to how we see or treat the disabled. Do we smile, look their way or pat them on the back? My husband has always been very good at these gestures, which has rewarded him with many return smiles of joy. I know he's aware of Galatians 6:10, "We must take advantage of every opportunity to show God's love through acts of kindness." We must remember the disabled as people with emotions, feelings, and the need for respect. Have you ever thought how you would handle a disabled child? I'm sure many pregnant women, their spouses, and grandparents have had those thoughts. My daughter during her four pregnancies was not pleased when others would state, "As long as the baby's healthy." She'd say to me, "I don't know why they say that?! This baby's going to have all of my love, healthy or not." She has four of the most beautiful children today! (Can you tell I'm their Mimi?)

In the following chapters we'll investigate and evaluate Ruthy's family dynamics and their reactions to Ruthy's disability and the wonderful environment that David knew.

3

Chapter 2

THE REST OF THE STORY

Before we explore David and Ruthy's disabilities, victories and their families, I would like to share a little about their city.

The real motivation for writing this book came from the heartwarming lives of David and Ruthy and their life lessons for us all. But as I revisited my hometown, I realized there are a few other valuable stories that should be written about Steubenville, Ohio – the city, its culture, the evolution of its reputation, and the effect on the city due to the closing of the steel mills.

Steubenville is a strong working class town in the Ohio Valley. It's made up of many ethnic mixes of many nationalities, surrounded and stabilized by the different church cultures.

My grandparents were part of the first group of settlers that were farming Germans. However, in my Steubenville days, the Italian culture became prominent in the area including DiCarlo's Pizza, Naples Spaghetti House, and Italian bread and rolls from Federico's (you can't get these anywhere else). My brother and I, as we visited as adults, couldn't get to these establishments fast enough. Of course, the Italian culture had more "angles" than just food?!

Before the Germans and the Italians, of course, the valley's original inhabitants were the Native American Indians. The area's Ohio River access was good for trade. It was also the path of George Washington's travels. His journal reports his camping there in 1770.[10]

In 1774, it was a group of men, the "Ohio Company", that were granted 500,000 acres of land from the King of England. That land

---

10   "Mingo Junction", by Larry Smith and Guy Mason

became Steubenville, Ohio. Two of those men were brothers of George Washington.[11]

President Washington may have been our first *name recognition* transient inhabitant, but you can't discuss Steubenville without mentioning its famous Dean Martin, Jimmy the Greek, and others mentioned throughout this book.

At present, the *name* of the day is Reno Saccoccia, the winningest coach in Steubenville High School history.

Coach Reno Saccoccia[12]

He was recently inducted into the Ohio High School Coaches Hall of Fame. Thirty-eight years of coaching with a record of 272 wins and 47 losses as a head coach! But to me, he was the very good, kind neighbor who watched over and visited my aging mother, Peggy Bair Reed. She thought it was the greatest blessing that a Steubenville Big Red coach would move in across the street. My mom lived with her great memories of being a Steubenville Big Red cheerleader.

When I mention football in Steubenville, I'm not talking about just a game, but an *institution* with a lot of gambling money riding on those Friday night games with full stadiums, and great celebrations. In the book,

---

11   Naples Spaghetti House Publication
12   Compliments of Reno Saccoccia

'Dino', "Dino started Steubenville High School which was known more for its football team The Big Red than for its academic standards." (1932)[13]

The high school has a weight room of equipment that would rival any college workout area that was donated by a non-Steubenville resident?! In the team locker room, posted on bricks of the wall are the players' names, number, and position they played since Big Red football started!

Their motto hanging on the weight room wall states, "When your memories are bigger than your dreams, you're in trouble." The first time I heard that motto, it was stated by the CEO of Pepsi! Big Red is serious about their winning! It's a fever!! I remember it well and still get goose bumps when I think of the great band dressed in black and red entering the stadium with sheer swing and soul, playing 'The Horse' (Big Red's mascot)! Football IS an *institution* in Steubenville!

I am sure the early settlers of the 1800's were thinking more of survival than football games. It is reported that these hardworking farmers with their families were frequented by missionaries evangelizing the valley. They established a German speaking Methodist Church, the first of many churches and denominations.

I am thankful that our family preserved for me a Lutheran German catechism book. It was the possession of my great-aunt who was a member of the last class of catechism that was taught in all German at Zion Lutheran Church.

The Graduates[14]

---

13   "Dino", Delta Biography
14   Compliments of the Harry Reed Family

At one point, the city was called the 'City of Churches'.[15] Those missionaries must have done a good job in winning souls for God, based on the number of church buildings?!

The current wave of evangelism in the last four decades is rooted in the works of the expanding world renowned Franciscan University of Steubenville. This fact would shock anyone who left the city before 1969!

As I was married in 1970 and revisited my hometown to attend my fifth class reunion, I was clueless to the spiritual effect of the university.

In retrospect, I did find out that many of our class "rascals" had become ministers! Plus I did note on church billboards that there were a lot of preachers' names ending in a vowel which were usually found in the Catholic Italian parishes.

When I really knew something was changing spiritually in Steubenville was when a visiting minister to our church in Toledo prayed for our pastor to see a revival of faith in Toledo as was happening in Steubenville, Ohio! My eyes popped open and my mouth fell open and my jaw dropped to the floor! Did he say "Steubenville?!" "My Steubenville?!" "Yes." He said, "Steubenville, Ohio!"

Franciscan University of Steubenville[16]

---

15   "Dino", Delta Biography
16   Compliments of the Franciscan University of Steubenville

Today as I sit in Steubenville's restaurants, it seems like the tables surrounding me are all having conversations about faith in their different churches! Now that's a switch!

This University enrichment to the city has been untapped for the city's much needed economic revival. There appears to be a great misunderstanding among some citizens due to the lack of religious tolerance or due to the lack of knowledge that the world's opinion of Steubenville has changed! That's an interesting study in itself.

Economic revival is desperately needed in the valley today due to the closings of the area steel mills. In 1970, Steubenville had the highest per capita income of any U.S. city.[17] Those citizens who have remained and watched a prosperous city of 50,000 residents decline to only 18,000 are to be commended. As fracking industry prospects are surfacing, Steubenville could become the restored, come back city of our era. At least Diane Sawyer said so in her ABC World News Tonight show on October 18, 2011.

There are many wonderful people who are trying to rebuild our once grand city. They have fought loss of income and heartbreak of their children leaving the area in a town where previously generations enjoyed each other for lifetimes. The mills were the glue for the past family closeness. Both David and Ruthy's families rode the *roller coaster* mill times. No mention of Steubenville can be told without the rise and fall of the steel mill industry.

Whatever past and present citizens know about their city of Steubenville, they may have missed the *reputation evolution* that has occurred around the world. Currently, Prince Sebastian of Luxembourg and his sister attend the University. There are students from every U.S. state and from many countries.

In 1969, as a student at Bowling Green State University, I was asked on a date by a good looking student, just back from Vietnam (now my husband of 42 years). Little did I know that he was concerned about dating me since I was from Steubenville! Our city's prostitution and gambling reputation had traveled far into his Navy circles. The seedy side of Steubenville was always our *claim to fame* – if you can call it that!

You can imagine my great surprise recently as in traveling the world over, the mention of my Steubenville roots makes eyes light up and people

---

17   "Let the Fire Fall", by Father Mike Scanlon

saying, "That wonderful, spiritual city, that amazing university on the hill! The city I didn't want to leave!"

Now that's a reputation evolution!! To quote the late Coach Abe Bryan (the "Father of Steubenville Football" per Coach Reno), at a banquet honoring Abe, "When I told people I was going to coach in Steubenville back in the early 60's, they would say, 'Ah, you're going to the city of gamblers and hookers!' Now in Florida when I mention Steubenville, they say, 'Ah, you're from that wonderful spiritual city with the great university on the hill'!"

Readers will hopefully gather some amazing insight into the city's reputation evolution, the hardships of the mill closings, and a glimpse of what Steubenville was and can become again with its hard working men and women who stayed in Steubenville, surviving or striving.

For now, let's together learn about David's and Ruthy's amazing triumphs and life lessons for us all. Enjoy the journey of David and Ruthy with their steel mill families who reside in the God Blessed city of Steubenville, Ohio.

Chapter 3

RUTHY'S ROOTS

Arch Rodgers was hot and sweaty as he came in from the farm that he and his Irish immigrant family farmed outside the small town of Bethany, West Virginia. He was going out that night with his beautiful gal, Birdie May Horner, from Wellsburg. There would be no pain left in him once he got a glance of the curvy body with the coal black hair. She had Indian and German blood in her. Not only was she striking, she was also strong. After the native Indians, the Germans were the original settlers and she was a fine blend of both.

He would brag to his buddies, "Now that Birdie May – she's a looker! I am going to marry that gal! Plus she's a good strong German." Everyone knew in the hills of West Virginia that the woman's job was to take care of her man, keep the cook stove fired up, raise the kids, and split and carry the wood to keep the house warm. So it was no wonder that Arch's drinking friends would lift up their mugs of beer in congratulations to him for his rare find. "Wow, can't beat that, Arch." they would proclaim in their toast.

The young Arch could never have imagined the family drama that history would record, as he knelt and told Birdie May that he wanted her to marry him and raise a family together. So it was that Arch Rodgers, at age 20, married Birdie Horner, only 17 years of age.

One thing they both agreed on was that they wanted better for their children. And for Arch Rodgers, there would be no more planting or working the fields.

Arch's brother, Ira, had gone to Morgantown to play football on a scholarship at West Virginia University. Little did Arch know that one day his brother, nicknamed *Rat* Rodgers, would be a Hall of Fame, college football legend. His name and plaque still hang in the halls of his alma mater. Nor did he know that for years, the youth of WVU would be affected positively as they were coached by their beloved and inspiring coach, *Rat* Rodgers.

Another brother of Arch's would become a Mormon minister. No one could figure that out, coming from his Irish Catholic family. The guys enjoyed their Saturday night (and other nights), as they journeyed to the pubs of Wellsburg, West Virginia. Their hometown of Bethany was a dry town. Never was it dry in Wellsburg, W. Va.! At 20 years old, Arch felt very confident that his painting job at Bethany College would be enough to support his family. Both he and Birdie agreed that even though he wouldn't make a lot of money, they would be able to send their children to college for free. Even though Arch suffered from asthma which was aggravated by his favorite Dutch Boy paint, he painted the college clock tower and all of Bethany College until he eventually retired.

Bethany College Clock Tower[18]

18   Compliments of Penny Smith

At Arch's proposal, Birdie said, "Yes!" to this hardworking Irish *fellar* that kept winking at her until he got her attention. He loved to whirl her around the dance halls of Wellsburg in their young years.

They were married by Rev. W. R. Moore at the Wellsburg Methodist Episcopal Church on May 15, 1907. Birdie was a strong, praying Christian who would make going to church a non-option for her brood! And brood she had! She attended the Bethany Disciples of Christ Church that was directly across from the college. Every Sunday in the Rodger's house, all seven of her children would be in Sunday school. As one daughter recalls, "Mom was easy on us, probably too easy, but going to Sunday school and church was non negotiable." Now Arch, he liked to listen to Father Goglin from Petersburg, West Virginia, on the radio.

Birdie's Church[19]

After the wedding, Arch and Birdie moved into a two bedroom home that would be theirs until they passed away. His only time away from his home was a short stay with his son and daughter-in-law during a sick spell. They lived in Macadoo Ridge, West Virginia, which was nestled in the hills between Bethany and Wellsburg.

---

19   Compliments of Penny Smith

Grandpa Arch and Grandma Birdie on their Front Porch[20]

"Two Bedrooms! Only two bedrooms!" It is the conversation of the family today. "Where did Grandma put all of them?" Those two bedrooms would eventually hold a total of 12 people!! There was Birdie and Arch's seven children, her daughter Naomi's two children, her daughter Ethel's one child, and of course, Arch and Birdie. Now that's a full house!! You wonder how they could have even conceived seven children in such small quarters. As I pondered this question, my husband said, "This is probably where the phrase, 'kids go outside and play' was coined!"

Birdie cooked on a cook stove fired up with coke. She'd stoke the fire early before anyone got up in the morning, and thus her day would start. She was cooking, doing laundry, mending, growing a huge garden, watching after ten children, and of course, taking care of Archie.

Once in awhile, after their son Andy married Odna, the whole gang would go to Odna's family fishing hole. These were Birdie's favorite times

– she stayed home!! Birdie could be seen using this quiet break to sit on their porch with her guitar, singing along with her favorite *Saturday Night Jamboree*. The whole family gathered on the porch every Saturday for this radio show. But no Saturday could compete with Birdie's only day off when the rest of the family went fishing!!

When Arch and Birdie's daughter described her parents to me, it finished the picture of the Rodger's household. "Dad was a non-educated, hard working, honest hillbilly. He had a violent Irish temper and could win any cursing contest! He was 'head of the house', sportsman, trapper, hunter, and fisherman. He possessed a knack for picking greens to cook and proudly took on that job."

The same daughter described her mother as a gentle, quiet woman who wore dresses everyday and a plat around her head. She cooked wonderful meals on her old cook stove, but proclaimed one of her most exciting days as the day she got her gas stove. She hummed hymns all day, prayed, read her Bible, went to church, and was baptized in Buffalo Creek.

Birdie May Rodgers[21]

21 Compliments of Ruthy Rodgers

Arch and Birdie had seven children; four boys and three daughters. Two daughters, Ethel and Naomi, brought home children for Grandma and Grandpa to raise. Ethel had a tragic life, and Naomi was the true *problem child.*

Backyard - Grandma Birdie and Two of her Grandchildren[22]

Along with their own seven children, Arch and Birdie accepted Ethel's first child into their home. Ethel had been expecting when she met her future husband, Tom. She was elated that he would marry her and take care of her and her baby boy. But after baby Gerald was born, Tom refused to let Gerald stay or ever come to their home. This was the first of Ethel's heartbreaks. But Gerald would be taken care of at Grandma and Grandpa's house.

Now daughter Naomi had been a problem for years. She quit school in the seventh grade and was given to thieving and lying from an early age. When her sisters were in school, Naomi would take their clothes and sell them. She loved gaudy jewelry and would use the money she made on selling the clothes to buy the jewelry. One morning, Birdie's wedding ring was gone. Everyone suspected Naomi. At first she repeatedly denied the theft, but eventually her story changed to having *buried it* and forgetting where it was buried. So Naomi's teenage and adult problems were no surprise for the Rodgers' family.

Before Naomi was married, she brought three children into the world, two for Grandma and Grandpa to raise. One of Naomi's sons was adopted by a Florida family cousin. One day that boy, working at a Florida Walgreens, was spotted by one of his unknown cousins. She recognized his name tag and invited him home to meet his birth mother. But there would be no grand family reunion when he visited. After a few encounters with his relatives, he got back in the car and sped to his home in Florida. Guess he didn't like what he saw. Surprised? Naomi's son eventually left Grandma's and was raised by his aunt.

Naomi was an interesting case. Naomi would bring one special child into Grandma's house and this little one was a girl, Ruthy.

Chapter 4

RUTH ELLEN RODGERS

On January 18, 1945 at the Wheeling, West Virginia Hospital, Naomi gave birth to a beautiful baby girl that would soon have the most beautiful green eyes and curly blond hair. Everyone who saw little Ruthy thought she was the most beautiful child they had ever seen!

Naomi stayed around for this child at Grandma's house. Ruthy was her beauty queen. Naomi would dress her up and parade around town with her, getting compliments on her beautiful daughter. Naomi even entered Ruthy in beauty pageants, which of course Ruthy won!

With all of the family at Grandma's house, Ruthy quickly became the center of attention. What Grandpa would not want his little granddaughter sitting on his lap? She was Grandma's little helper in the kitchen and in the garden. Ruthy had eyes that twinkled and a smile that would win you over no matter what child mischief she encountered - who could discipline this precious little cherub?

It was right after winning a beauty contest that little Ruthy found herself burning up with fever, lying on the couch. Grandma didn't panic because she had nursed many a fever with cold rags. But it wasn't long until it became obvious that Ruthy was very sick. The discussion of going to a hospital never came up because in the hills of West Virginia, you just didn't go to the hospital for a fever! Day after day, night after night, Grandma sat by little Ruthy's bedside. Ruthy's beautiful green eyes raged with fever and eventually started staring into space. Soon her little body was wrenching with spasms and the realization that she needed hospital care became obvious.

As the doctors cared for Ruthy, it was determined that she had contracted the dreaded disease of spinal meningitis. She was suffering petit mall seizures and at this point had suffered extreme damage to her entire left side, brain, and limbs.

Leg Braces for Ruthy[23]

Grandpa would make regular trips to Steubenville to get medicine and Grandma would pray over her little angel. In those days, with delayed treatment, Ruthy's life expectancy was deemed to be months or at best, a few years. It was decided that the doctor's recommendation for physical therapy and treatment at the Shriners Hospital would not be heeded. Grandma would take care of her baby at home.

Ruthy's Bedroom at Grandma's[24]

23 Compliments of Penny Smith
24 Compliments of Ruthy Rodgers

Of course, no longer having her *beauty queen*, Naomi was gone. Caregiving wasn't Naomi's style of living.

There would be no more school for Ruthy. Her mobility being untreated and the school stairways not handicap friendly made furthering her education impossible. But Ruthy would eventually teach herself to read and write.

Ruthy was always proud of her coat that matched Grandma's. She would get excited to wear it on Sunday to go to church.

The Matching Coats[25]

---

25 Compliments of Ruthy Rodgers

Backyard With Grandma[26]

With all of Grandma's caring, there came a time when Grandma needed the care. Everyone remembers the chilling diagnosis of breast cancer! For Ruthy, she could not imagine being without her grandmother. Even though she fought for four years, the day came when Birdie May Horner Rodgers was no longer there to take care of little Ruthy. She was thirteen years old and totally unable to care for herself. Her aunt came to Naomi with the invitation for Ruthy to live with her in Macadoo Ridge. So at the age of 13, she left the only home she had ever known and went to *boot camp* at her aunt's. No more pampering because her aunt could see Ruthy's potential. The tying of shoes and all personal hygiene were new to Ruthy, since Grandma had literally taken care of Ruthy as an invalid.

Ruthy noticed after a few months that her aunt wasn't feeling very well. Every morning, she would be very sick. It was soon announced that her aunt was pregnant! Within months, she was ordered to full bed rest, so mother Naomi was summoned to come for Ruthy. All expected Ruthy's return.

---

26   Compliments of Penny Rodgers

Naomi, after three children out of wedlock, had married and had a new baby, Rusty. She lived in Mingo, overlooking the Ohio River skyline of billowing smoke stacks and dirty steel mills. Her husband, Russell, worked in the mills and Naomi had finally settled down. With all the adjustments that Ruthy had to make over the last few years, she was more than excited to make this move to her own mother's home! She would have her mom, stepdad, and a little baby brother.

Ruthy and her Mom[27]

Ruthy had barely slept the night before, with the excitement of seeing her mom the next morning. She had hobbled around, gathering her things together, awaiting the car to pull into the driveway! Naomi finally arrived and Ruthy couldn't smile any brighter as she embraced her mother. It had been a long time since Grandma's funeral, which was the last time Ruthy had seen her mother. As usual, Naomi's greeting was cold and less than welcoming, but for Ruthy it was the happiest day of her life! Home with her mom and part of her own family.

---

27 Compliments of Ruthy Rodgers

For three days she felt a joy she hadn't known since Grandma was ill. So when Naomi came to wake Ruthy, she thought nothing of her mom's directives to dress *real pretty* because they were going to take a trip. "Wow, a vacation!" Naomi packed Ruthy's small suitcase and helped her dress. "Where are we going Mom?" Ruthy asked. "Just hurry Ruthy." was the only response.

It had been less than a week since Ruthy had settled into her mom's house – and now she was on a vacation! After two hours in the car they wound down a long, treed lane. "Boy this sure is a big place." said Ruthy. And it was big! It was the *Ohio Institute for the Insane*! At this point, Ruthy could not read the sign, but a horrible feeling of dread swept over her as she got out of the car. When Naomi took Ruthy's suitcase and walked her up to the door, Russ and Rusty stayed in the car.

Ruth's New Home[28]

A few minutes later, Naomi had signed some papers, handed Ruthy over to the nurse, and walked out of Ruthy's life for what would be 22 years! Her aunt had expected Ruthy to return to her once her son was born, but Naomi said Ruthy was in a school in Columbus. No one knew what had happened to Ruth Ellen Rodgers.

---

28 Google, scanned by Patrick J. Hall

Recently, in the writing of this book, we asked Ruthy's aunts where Ruthy was in Columbus. No one had any idea. One aunt said, "All she knew was that one day at the Ohio State Fair when she and her husband had taken Naomi with them, they had a chance encounter with Ruthy on the midway. Her *school* evidently had an outing at the fair. There stood Ruthy with her estranged mother, face to face. Other than that sighting, Naomi never mentioned Ruthy." The aunts were certain that Naomi surely couldn't have put Ruthy in an institute for the insane! But as we checked out details and later showed Ruthy pictures, she emphatically picked the institute picture as her home from 1957 to 1979. When asked questions about those years, Ruthy prefers not to give any specifics. Those years weren't good memories. Conditions were found to be so bad in the Ohio State Institution that it was closed. After the institute, Ruthy went to live for four years with Mrs. Howard who had worked at the institute and had a crippled child who needed care. When the institute closed, Mrs. Howard took in several girls as a paid foster care giver. The girls were also asked to help care for her invalid son. This arrangement lasted only four years as Mrs. Howard had gotten ill and could no longer qualify to be a care giver.

Due to this, Mrs. Howard called Naomi and was quite surprised to hear that Naomi didn't want her daughter.

Ruthy was unwanted!

Chapter 5

COUSIN PENNY

As Penny went through her mail that morning, she stared at the envelope with a Columbus postmark. Penny was 30 years old, had three boys, a husband she never loved, and not much of a life. In a cramped three bedroom house where she lived with her husband of 14 years, she was making important decisions about changing her own situation.

Penny With Another Sad Holiday[29]

Nonchalantly, she ripped open the envelope, pulled out the half sheet of lined paper and observed the scribblings of her cousin, Ruthy. What a shock!! She had not seen or heard from her in years – 22 years! Truth be told, no one knew where poor little Ruthy had been for years.

29 Compliments of Penny Smith

Ethel (Penny's Mom) and Penny's Last Time with Ruthy for Over 22 Years[30]

As Penny's eyes read through the few words, she felt the tinge of pain remembering her own *homeless* fears in her upbringing. "Ruthy needs a place to live!"

Only could a woman with the heart of Penny and memories of her own abandonment respond so quickly to Ruthy's plea for help. Yes, she would go get her! After a phone conversation with Naomi, and her husband's okay, it was determined that, yes, Penny would go pick up Ruthy from her foster home in Columbus, Ohio. She would take care of her in their already small, crowded home. Incidentally, Penny's home in Mingo was just down the street from Ruthy's mother, Naomi. Even though Naomi never wanted the responsibility of being a mother to Ruthy, she had no trouble telling everyone else what to do with and for Ruthy! Poor Penny!

---

30 Compliments of Penny Smith

Naomi Visits Ruthy at Penny's[31]

Our Penny, so precious, sweet, attractive, and caring, never knew during her childhood what rental or what city she would be living in from week to week. Would there by any food or heat for the family? Her mother, Ethel, was one of Grandma Birdie's seven children. Grandma raised Ethel's firstborn, Gerald. Penny's dad wanted nothing to do with Gerald. Even though he married Ethel knowing the baby she was carrying wasn't his, he never would let Gerald in his home.

Tom, Penny's dad, was a character – a bad character! He was from Wellsburg, West Virginia, and had met Ethel in Wellsburg. He was a hard drinking mechanic that could never hold a job. He would run up bills in one city, get evicted, and move to another town.

Even though Ethel loved Tom, most of Penny's memories of her mother were of her tears from crying most of the night. Knowing her father's love for her mother, how could Ethel have been so blind as to marry Tom, a womanizer and drunkard?! He left the family often and ventured to his mistress Delores in Canton. Everyone knew. Even Ethel and the children

31 Compliments of Ruthy Rodgers

knew. When Tom was home, it wasn't a pretty site. He was abusive to his wife and his children.

Tom[32]

But what could Ethel do with six children to care for under her roof? Even though Tom refused to raise Ethel's son, he was in favor of giving Ethel another mouth to feed with her sister Naomi's son! So Ethel raised six children, but not her own first born son.

Penny's world at nine years old started crashing down when in September of 1961, her beloved mother was diagnosed with cervical cancer! How much more could her mother take or for that matter, how much more could Penny take?

With his lack of character, Tom thought his wife's illness and six children to care for were great reasons to call upon his sisters, Liz and Alice, for help. He dropped his family off at Alice's house, assuring her he would pay rent. The family moved into a front section of her house. Of course, no rent was ever paid and Tom left town to be with his mistress in Canton!

---

32   Compliments of Penny Smith

Penny's Aunt Alice's Home[33]

Penny remembers the agony of her ninth year. They spent their mom's last Christmas together with their father gone, no heat, no food, and their mom sobbing with heartache and pain. Her bed was in the kitchen with the stove door left open for their only heat. Penny remembers spending the day with her mom crying and apologizing for having no food. That's not a Christmas Penny likes to remember.

In the following months, their dad would show up once each month to get commodities from the Salvation Army and bake some bread to leave with the children.

The sights and sounds are still vivid in Penny's mind of when she was awakened to the blood curdling screams of her sister. They were coming from downstairs. Penny started to run down the steps only to be held back as her older brother Tommy's loving arms wrapped around her to stop her. He held her on the staircase to protect her from the scene. Penny cried in her brother's arms.

The screams had come as her sister witnessed the gushing blood pouring from her mother. The sight was gruesome. Soon the funeral home hearse would come to take Ethel to the hospital. Karen was left to care for their mother by herself during Ethel's last few days when they let her come home from the hospital. It took Karen many alcoholic years to get over

---

33 Compliments of Penny Smith

those days. Penny at age nine, found herself living alone when her mom was in the hospital She decided to go to Aunt Liz's to stay.

She found herself restless and wanting to return to where her family was staying, which was at her Aunt Alice's home. Liz did not want Penny returning to Alice's, probably due to Penny's fragile emotions at the time. As Penny defied her Aunt Liz's commands not to go, Aunt Liz could be heard yelling, "If you go, you ain't coming back!" And so Penny never went to Aunt Liz's again.

During that horrid year, Penny remembers the extreme kindness shown to her by her teacher, Mrs. Legitt. This was Penny's only kindness that year. Imagine being nine years old and all this pain surrounding you?!

Tom was not at home, of course, when Ethel died in March of 1962. He returned for the burial on April 2nd in Wellsburg. Unknown to Penny, Ethel had asked her sister to take care of Penny after she died. So as everyone was congregated together after the funeral, Tom pointed to Penny and said, "There she is." And that fast, with a terrible shock, Penny was torn from her father and siblings. At age nine, she was without her mom and the family was falling apart. Penny would turn ten on June 1st.

So again Penny changed schools and was enrolled into a new grade school. Her aunt was the mother of three little boys. How special Penny felt as her aunt dressed her in all new pretty clothes. Penny was a real darling and covered up her aching heart with her warm smile. Having only been in school for one month, she was honored with being May Queen. She had no idea about her title and had to ask, "What is a May Queen?" "It's going to be alright." she thought. She found herself in a new and warm environment with new friends, new clothes, food, and a clean bed of her own!

Boy was she wrong! The next two years of her life, she looks back on now with sheer dread. During those years in Irondale, Ohio, her only good memories were her times spent next door with her uncle's mother. There she could laugh, play games, swing on Grandma's swing and totally feel safe. She went to Grandma's any chance she could get.

After two years, Penny found the circumstances so unbearable that at 12 years old, she bolted from the house and ran away. The police and a fireman located her at midnight. She was taken back to her nightmare. This occurred in October, and her aunt realized by May that Penny's father needed to come get her. And he did!

Penny's dad was used to moving, so he and his wife Delores picked up Penny and moved back to Canton. Tom had married Delores three months after Ethel had passed away. Only three months and his mistress for years became his wife! Right after the funeral, Tom had abandoned all and taken Delores to Florida. All was well with self-centered Tom, but he left children with shambled lives, especially his girls. Jenny was in reform school for stealing, Karen wandered the streets until her boyfriend's family took her to live with them, and Penny was in her nightmare.

Now Penny was living in Canton, Ohio with two alcoholics. They only lasted in Canton for one year. Penny's brother Tommy had married Beverly and had a house in Wellsburg, W. Va. So Tom decided to move in with them.

As the beginning of the school year drew closer, Penny needed to register again in a new school. In the process of registering for junior high in Wellsburg, Penny's mother's information was requested. Tom absolutely refused to give school authorities any information on his deceased wife. No problem, he just decided to pack up and move to Mingo, Ohio. He moved directly across from Naomi, his former sister-in-law and Ruthy's mom.

So Penny started her junior high school years in Mingo Junction, Ohio. Mingo is three miles from Steubenville and used to be part of Steubenville Township. Like Steubenville, it is along the Ohio River. Penny's new home was perched up on a steep hill called Deandale Hill, which overlooked the smoke stacks and dirt of the steel mills.

Steel Mill Smog and Dirt[34]

34 Compliments of Penny Smith

This area often was called Gobbler's Nob because the river bank is steep, rocky and cragged. Most people have never seen dirt like the dirt from a steel mill town. When I resided there, I went to a black stone church. Our wedding pictures taken in 1970 are proof of that black stone, but today because of sandblasting, the church is a beautiful white stone church.

Soot Covered Church[35]

Same Church After Sandblasting[36]

---

35 Compliments of the Harry Reed Family
36 Compliments of Zion Lutheran Church

A white sweater would turn gray in a day. On my first visit home from college, I remarked "What is that haze hanging over the city?" Dirt was just part of the territory. If you would ask the unemployed steel workers at the USWA office what they think about the clean air now, they would tell you they preferred the dirty air when they could feed their families. The city has dwindled to 18,000 people from 50,000. I believe the whole town would all have that same opinion.

But when Penny lived on Gobbler Nob, the soot and smoke was billowing out of those stacks. The houses built on the hills of Mingo faced the mill where noon whistles and emergency sirens were daily sounds. Those dreaded emergency sirens halted all breathing as you knew some friend or neighbor could have just died in a hot vat of steel.

Naomi's house backed up to Gobbler's Nob on Locust Street, and Tom's *shack* was just across the street. That dead-end street was to represent many more unpleasant places for Penny in the future. But for now, Penny lived with her dad and started jr. high in Mingo. Delores and Tom worked in Wellsburg. She didn't see them much and when she did, they were drunk.

The river valley was inhabited with hard working people, unlike her father. These people carry on the torch of the American Founding Fathers with their Judeo Christian work ethic. It was a hard steel mill life in order to earn money to take care of their families. These river valley inhabitants centered their lives around their families and their churches. These towns are made up of diverse immigrants, arriving from many ethnic and religious backgrounds. The area has been known to be called *the league of nations*. These fathers wanted to do whatever was necessary to give their children better lives. The root of the valley's school philosophy is that their children deserve the very best possible. Fathers worked hard, long hours mostly in unsafe environments in the mills.[37] In this town where *children were prized and* cared *for*, imagine our little Penny going to school with children from close families, while her father was probably at Dugan's with its nightly mix of 8 or 9 ball and lots of drinking. Dugan's was an *institution* in the valley for 60 years Of course, typical of that area, there was small time (and some big time) gambling. Long before the lottery, it was a daily activity for most to stop into Dugan's to buy a betting number

---

37   :"Mingo Junction", by Larry Smith and Guy Mason

before going home. Betting was done on everything. One of my cousin's jobs in high school was to run down to the cigar store and buy numbers for the boss everyday. And at Christmas, if the boss got cigarettes instead of liquor from the bookies – the boss would march him right back to insist on the bottle of liquor for the holidays, received by the higher rolling gamblers. It was the culture.

Dugan's[38]

Dugan's[39]

---

38 Courtesy Paula (Kendrach) Kopcha
39 Courtesy Paula (Kendrach) Kopcha

Interestingly, along with this culture, the many ethnic churches of Mingo represented the social life of the family. The different church social lives maintained their own ethnic culture. It was first the Methodist missionaries who settled there and built the Methodist Episcopal Church. Then came the Catholic Mission movement. Next were all the other diverse churches and cultures:

- Slovak Presbyterian
- Russian Orthodox
- Greek Catholic
- Serbian Eastern Orthodox
- Byzantine Catholic
- Harmony Methodists
- First Baptist
- First United Presbyterian
- Methodist Church[40]

Almost sounds like God's confused. Which I doubt! The valley was once known as the valley of churches. In a steel mill town, one had to be tolerant of these different ethnic groups. Their lives could depend on another ethnic group working beside them in the coal mines, steel mills, and railroads.

But as all these close families and church cultures were socializing, a lonely 13 year old girl lived up on the hill with two alcoholics. Her life was social in wrong areas as she was an *old* 13, having taken care of herself most of her life as she survived.

After one weekend of Delores's and Tom's binge drinking, Penny awoke on Sunday morning to even more yelling and fighting than normal. Her dad was rummaging through Delores's purse shouting, "Where's the money?" Of course he had forgotten that it had all gone to drinking and partying all weekend. He was so mad that he threw a shoe at Delores and started towards her in anger! Penny stepped between them to save Delores and broke up the fight. Her dad stormed out of the house. That was Delores's last Sunday morning with Tom or any morning with Tom. Little did Penny know that it would also be her last Sunday morning with her father. Delores packed up her belongings and was gone by nightfall before Tom arrived back home.

---

40 "Mingo Junction", by Larry Smith and Guy Mason

Penny cautiously got up Monday morning, worried about the climate of the home. Fortunately Tom was asleep, so Penny readied herself for school as she did every school day. She jumped on the school bus and thought to herself, "Well, no more Delores." She finished her day at school and rode home on the bus. She always walked up the hill from the bus stop, leaving off other students at difference places on the hill, until she reached her street at the very top. All of a sudden she became startled at the sight of her dad backing out of their driveway with all of his belongings packed to the top of the car. He tried to be gone before she came home, but he hadn't made it. He rolled down the window and said, "I am moving to Florida, do you want to go?" Penny stared at this selfish man, and at 15 years old, decided to stay. She remembers walking up the drive to an empty house. With much confusion she walked over to her cousin's house, and announced, "Can I live with you, my dad is gone." They said "We know." They provided her with a roof over her head. Even though he was her cousin, he had lived with them as a brother since Naomi didn't want to raise her son and Grandma had passed away. He was Ruthy's half brother. He welcomed his *little sister* (cousin) into their already crowded home. At least she didn't have to change schools. Penny made a conscious decision during those rough years of the 60's to honor her mother's memory by not getting into drinking, drugs, or smoking. In just ten short years of being with her mother, her mom's example and prayers were honored by Penny. I am sure her mom didn't realize the possible pitfalls in Penny's life since she thought all would be taken care of with Penny at her aunt's.

As she settled in, things started unraveling in that home. Her cousin took to running with a very tough motorcycle gang and would come home drunk. Once home, he would beat his wife. Their daughter still remembers the blood. It wasn't long until the cheating started and the fireworks began! So a divorce and another loss of home clouded over Penny.

Penny's only hope, at the age of 16, was to say yes to Bob's proposal. Bob was 26! They ran off to Wheeling with a fake identification prepared by a family member. No love, just a roof over her head! She was trapped!

Married Penny[41]

Shortly after they were married, Penny remembers looking out of their Steubenville apartment on Adam Street one hot summer day. She watched the civil rights march below! It was a *hot* summer in Steubenville in July, 1968, as non-residents had poured into the city with their threats of burning down Steubenville.

"The trouble had started in Weirton, West Virginia, just across the river from Steubenville. Steubenville and Weirton are actually one city with the Ohio River flowing down the middle. Incredibly, for a northern state two years after passage of the civil rights bill, the Weirton Community Center had a policy against interracial dancing. The preceding night the manager of the center ejected a young black man for dancing with a young white woman. Angry black youths and others not so young marched down the street to the police station to complain. Nervous police watched the demonstration from inside the station. Then they put on riot gear and rushed into the crowd busting heads. The rest of it followed: looting of

---

41   Compliments of Ruthy Rodgers

stores, random vandalism, arson, wholesale arrests of black youths, angry denunciations of blacks by whites and vice versa.

Rumors made a bad situation much worse. In fact, the rioting that went on in people's minds was much worse than the rioting on the streets of Weirton. It was reported that carloads of blacks armed with rifles were roaming white neighborhoods, and that white gangs were looking for blacks to kill, and that the police had beaten up little black kids. The latest report had it that black gangs were coming across the river the next night to burn down the city of Steubenville."[42]

Penny was scared like the rest of the Steubenville residents. But her thoughts drifted to her own unfair lack of freedom. She was 17, no high school diploma, no driver's license, pregnant and in a hot apartment with a man she didn't love. This scenario reminds me of Dick Vermeil's (super bowl coach) comment, "Eventually everyone has to sit down to life's banquet of consequences." Penny was definitely sitting at her untasty banquet. Her freedom would come much later than the freedom fighters down on the street!

Since Penny was pregnant, the decision was made to move back to Mingo and move in with Bob's brother and sister-in-law. So back to Gobbler's Nob they went. Mike had two children and two bedrooms! So all six lived together while Bob built his bride, Penny, a block home behind his brother's house. Before the block house was finished, Bob and Penny had their first son, Bobby, on December 1, 1968. This now made it seven people in the two bedroom home. They were ready to move into their cinder block, one bedroom home as Penny found out that she was pregnant again! As they moved into the damp block building with no insulation, only a heating stove, no air conditioning or windows, and a pipe shower, Penny was miserable. As she recalls this period in her life, the tears roll down her face and the panic strikes, to where she can't continue to communicate.

Penny had horrible living conditions, an abusive husband that she didn't love, his family surrounding her, and no where to go for support. She resigned herself in a numb emotional condition that these circumstances were her plight in life! Her only glimmer of hope was that this time she really felt that she was going to have a girl! She was excited – her *good*

---

42 "Let The Fire Fall", by Father Mike Scanlon

buddy, family friend for life was about to come into her world. They would call her Jamie. So with a few pink items, Penny waited and focused on her little Jamie.

Little Jamie was born December 26, 1969, and died December 26, 1969. She lived only 20 minutes. Penny was heartbroken as she went home to her cold block house. In 1970, she was pregnant with another boy, Scott, who was born in 1971. Penny was now 20 with three pregnancies behind her and two boys under the age of two! She could not figure out how she had let herself get to this point. Penny had mistrusted men all her life, understandably so, from her many bad experiences. She had married, not for love, but for a roof over her head! Then in 1972, she had one more son, Mark.

It was at this point that she decided to pursue her GED Certificate. She hoped that this effort at education might bring her freedom. However, that didn't quite fit into Bob's *barefoot and pregnant* plan. Several relatives of Bob's were going to GED classes which sparked Penny's interest. She so wanted to attend the course to get a high school diploma. Bob absolutely refused her intentions. She was *forbidden* to attend. But Penny privately and secretively studied at home. She was able to slip out and take the test, passing it the first time.

From that moment on, Penny's dream for a better life began. She thought, "No more cheating, abusive husband – no more isolation and loneliness." Penny would be free to start over!

Chapter 6
RUTHY GOES TO PENNY'S

At this time in her life when Penny was planning her own freedom, she knew she had to take on the responsibility of Ruthy. She knew the panic of being without a roof over her head and without a home.

Ruthy heard Dorothy Howard say, "Ruthy you have a call from a Penny." Ruthy couldn't get out of her chair fast enough! She hobbled over to the phone as fast as she could and her eyes lit up as she heard Penny say, "Ruthy, its ok. I'm coming to get you."

And so it was that Ruthy returned to Mingo, Ohio. But this time she would live with her cousin Penny and her husband, and their three little boys.

Ruthy's New Family[43]

Ironically, Penny lived down the street from Naomi with her husband and one child! Naomi finally decided to raise one of the children she birthed. She was still giving this boy a large baby bottle with a large nipple for lunch when he came home from school at the age of six years old! Naomi was not the *mother of the year*!

When Ruthy moved in to stay with Penny, Penny gave Ruthy her own room which Ruthy called her butterfly room. Penny had been kind enough to have decorated the new room with lots of color and with butterfly wallpaper. Penny's husband, Bob, readied the room in their small home for Ruthy. For Bob that room meant Penny would have to stay with him in order to give Ruthy a home. But for Ruthy, this room was a dream come true – *a real room of her own*!

Ruthy's Butterfly Room[44]

Penny never would take any of Ruthy's social security money. And of course, Naomi never thought or cared to help pay for the decorations for the room or for any of her daughter's care. Naomi had never been able to manage money – her sister reported to me that Naomi often called and requested funds. Even in her later years, Naomi would call the bank each

44 Compliments of Penny Smith

day to find out her financial balances and then she would spend the *balance* that day. Naomi had no concept that she had already written checks which had not yet cleared, and would need those funds in her bank account.

Penny's youngest child was seven when Ruthy came to stay. Only years later did Penny hear of the tricks her three boys played on Ruthy. Ruthy smiles when Penny says, "Why didn't you tell me?" Ruthy answers with a big grin, "I didn't want to get them in trouble!!!" Ruthy was even known to pick up candy and treats for Penny's boys. She likes to say, "I spoiled them!"

Both Naomi's husband Russell, and Penny's husband, Bob, worked in the steel mills at the bottom of the hill behind Naomi's house. Bob worked at the 80" hot strip mill which was a rough, dirty, and a hot-hot-hot job! So Penny was never surprised at Bob's stops after work with the buddies. They started lasting longer. She was just as glad not to have Bob around. When he was home, there were fights – mean, hard fights. There were Penny's true accusations of Bob's unfaithfulness and Bob's jealous accusations of Penny entertaining men or even looking into a man's face. Penny had spent her married life looking down at the ground when she was in public. Of course, never was she out in public without Bob. She truly was captive.

With all the fighting in the home, Ruthy would retreat to her room as Penny's sons would also scatter to avoid the fights. Ruthy wondered how long she would be able to sleep with her little butterflies! Her greatest fears came when her mother Naomi would come from across the street. Even though Naomi didn't want to raise Ruthy nor care for her nor financially support her, or even show love to her, Naomi had very strong opinions of what Penny should do for Ruthy.

You would only have to meet Penny once to know that only the beautiful, kind Penny could have tolerated Naomi. Of course, once your mother has abandoned you for 22 years, you would always be afraid of her intentions every time she came through the door.

Penny had watched Ruthy and realized that Ruthy had taught herself to read and write, and was obviously advanced in her capabilities. Ruthy managed her small social security funds better than Naomi handled her own household budget.

Penny always had Ruthy's best interest in mind. Her only concern for Ruthy was that she saw how bored Ruthy was after six months of being cooped up at Penny's. Penny could relate as she had been couped up for thirteen years! It was with these thoughts in her mind that Penny's eyes opened wide when she read in the Herald Star Newspaper about a workshop for individuals with developmental disabilities.

At the very mention of being out in public, Ruthy recoiled. "What was Penny thinking?" she thought. "I am disabled, crippled, shy, and afraid." were the thoughts going through Ruthy's mind like a broken CD playing the same words over and over again. But Penny was convinced that Ruthy could do this and that they should check out Jeff Co.

Penny fought an uphill battle, not only with Ruthy, but of course with Naomi. Naomi thought Penny had lost her mind to send *my innocent little unprotected darling into the world of wolves.* Naomi would say this repeatedly to anyone who would listen. Of course, these dialogues did nothing to calm Ruthy's fears. But Penny knew the only thing that can overcome fear is action – and Penny needed to make Ruthy act!

When Penny was convinced that Jeff Co. was a sound and safe place for Ruthy to work, she *pushed* Ruthy onto the workshop bus and totally ignored Naomi. Ruthy today will say this was one of the most important *shoves* of her life.

Ruthy's Award[45]

---

45 Compliments of Ruthy Rodgers

Chapter 7
Ruthy Goes to Work

Thank goodness for the dedication of organizations such as JeffCo Inc. and taxpayers who have advanced the care and provisions for the mentally disabled. JeffCo is the adult division of the Jefferson County Board of Developmental Disabilities. The philosophy is that a job with pay adds to self respect in society. These types of facilities provide a sheltered, but realistic work environment. This is just what Ruthy needed at this point in her life. The major goal at JeffCo is to elevate the level of physical, mental, social and vocational efficiency to acquire and maintain skills that will assist an individual to live independently.

The free programs of our society are extremely burdensome to U.S. taxpayers. But never do I pass up the opportunity to mark *yes* when a levy is requested for the developmentally disabled. I believe when *giveaways* started they were meant to be primarily for people who truly need help! In considering the current political atmosphere of redistributing wealth, I am of the opinion that what is really needed is the redistribution of the handouts. Not giving subsidies to encourage teen girls to become early mothers but rather helping those developmentally disabled, should be considered.

I was recently reminded of the pain, costs, and emotional dynamics of a situation when a friend of mine in California with a 22 year old developmentally disabled daughter relayed this story. One day when at her daughter's school for those with development disabilities, a disabled 12 year old boy with brain damage, sitting in a wheelchair, asked her, "Was your daughter born like this?" He said, "I wasn't. I was in a car accident two years ago." That boy and his family really need our help!

So JeffCo was the perfect answer of help for Ruthy. Penny registered Ruthy, hoping she would gain confidence and strength in making decisions through her experiences at the workshop. Of course, Ruthy was very shy and very scared at the thought of her JeffCo *experience*. Mother Naomi didn't help the situation with her vocal protests about Ruthy's inadequacies and inabilities. Naomi was sure that Ruthy did not have the talents, skills, or mental capacity to work at the workshop. She emphasized Ruthy's shyness and physical vulnerability due to her physical disability. Penny would not listen to Naomi's whining or Ruthy's fears and went forward with enrolling Ruthy at JeffCo.

The beginning of Ruthy's work life transition was rough. Penny wondered if she had done the right thing when the fights started over Bill. Ruthy, out in the world, had fallen for a fellow worker. As a case worker told me, "Even though a developmentally disabled person has mental challenges, they have hormones, emotional needs, etc. as we all have." But Ruthy's first attachment was a bad one. This Bill had issues – bad issues!

Penny forbade this relationship and kept a diligent watch over the situation. She informed the workshop of her concerns. It was at this time that Penny encountered a very fine man, Ed Kelps, who was President of the JeffCo Parents Association. Ed was aware of Penny's reports and investigated the situation. Almost immediately the problem was resolved and Bill was no longer accepted at JeffCo. Penny was very appreciative and thought a lot of Ed Kelps.

As Ruthy was feeling more comfortable with her job and no longer mad at Penny, she looked forward to the bus ride and the busy day she would have with all her new friends. Penny's tough love had paid off.

One day when Ruthy came home from work, she said, "Somebody at JeffCo likes me." Penny's heart skipped a beat and she immediately dropped what she was doing and sat to talk with Ruthy. "Well, what's he like?" Penny asked with her voice a little shaky. Ruthy replied, "He's real tall. When Arrell introduced us, I had to look way up." She continued, "Some of the girls told me, 'He is too big for you. He is going to hurt you'." That's all Penny needed to hear to confirm her fears. "I don't know about this, Ruthy. It doesn't sound like a good idea to be friends with this big man." Penny warned. But Ruthy beamed and said, "You know what he said to me?" He said, "Ruthy I not going to hurt you, I going to spoil you!" "Oh really?" Penny thought and then asked his name. When Ruthy said "David Kelps!" Penny's shoulders relaxed for the first time during this conversation. Ed Kelps' son, OK!!! She had never seen David, but she knew his dad enough to know he would be a good choice.

Within a few weeks, Penny invited David to come for dinner. She was busy at the sink when David's dad dropped him off in the driveway. As Ruthy ushered him into the kitchen, he stepped right behind Penny at the sink and gave her one of his famous, friendly bear hugs! She jumped, turned around and screamed! In shock, she saw a seven foot, 330 pound *giant* standing in her kitchen, smiling down at her from ear to ear! After her heart stopped pounding, she welcomed Ruthy's friend. Her thoughts were, "*Tall guy* is not the right term for David Kelps and I sure hope he doesn't want to hurt Ruthy!"

Of course, Ruthy was proud as punch of her new *feller*. During dinner, in walked you-know-who from down the street – Naomi. She entered without knocking, hands on her hips and said, "Why wasn't I told about this?" She highly, verbally disapproved and wanted to make sure that everyone knew her opinion. She told Penny that this is why she didn't want Ruthy at JeffCo. She immediately didn't like David and that opinion never changed.

It wasn't long after that explosive night that Ruthy approached Penny about moving out on her own. Penny could just imagine Naomi's reaction to this news! But Ruthy had done her homework. She assured Penny of her case worker's willingness to find her a place to live. Penny knew Ruthy managed her money well, so she started to consider the move. Both Penny and Ruthy also knew that Penny's marriage wouldn't last much longer. With Penny's GED in hand, she had fought the battle with Bob and gotten her driver's license and started working. Bob's normal *rants* were becoming louder and much more frequent. It was just a matter of time.

Penny's Unhappiness Showed![46]

Against Naomi's wishes again, Penny walked Ruthy through her next steps towards becoming independent. They found her an apartment where she could walk to the store and where there was security at night. Penny asked Ruthy the very sensitive and controversial question, "Ruthy do you ever want to care for children?" With Ruthy's "No." answer, arrangements were made and the State of Ohio paid the bill. So Ruthy ventured into life on her own. With Naomi kicking and screaming, she and her husband went with Penny to move Ruthy into the previous Fort Steuben Hotel which had been turned into government housing in Steubenville. Of course, they enlisted the help of big Dave for the move. David's family, the givers that they are, of course, caringly helped also. Naomi's husband set up a CB radio for Ruthy in her new apartment. Both he and David loved their times on the CB. Now Ruthy could also communicate through the CB band. After Ruthy was set up in her apartment, she only had one visit from Penny and her Mom. She couldn't get them out of her apartment fast enough! Not because of Penny of course, but she didn't trust Naomi one bit. It would be thirty years until Penny would see Ruthy again.

---

46 Compliments of Ruthy Rodgers

Ruthy's First Apartment[47]

Ruthy thrived at JeffCo! The following picture and newspaper article from the Steubenville Herald Star shows how *insecure Ruthy* has become *confident Ruthy* in her own element. As you read this article, remember this is the woman who spent 22 years in a *home for the insane* and was thought to be totally useless by her mother!

An article written about Ruthy for the Steubenville Herald Star Newspaper:

> Ruth Ellen enjoys living on her own in a one-bedroom apartment in the city's south end. She explains that her home was partially furnished by friends and she is especially pleased with the new washer and dryer given to her by her church.

> Ruth Ellen was normal to the age of 4 when she contracted spinal meningitis which ultimately damaged her brain. She is considered high functional and capable of managing her own affairs. At 45, she has no desire to live in a semi-structured environment or with family. She is very happy to be on her own and has no fear.

---

47   Compliments of Ruthy Rodgers

Ruth Ellen lives in an apartment complex, which, according to Mehalik is usually how most independent living facilities are structured.

"At first I was worried about money, but I had the chance and I really wanted to do it." Ruth Ellen said. "I learned how to manage. First, you pay your rent and your bills, then you can do what you want."

But Ruth Ellen has no interest in working outside of the School of Bright Promise or JeffCo Workshop and feels that going into an inpatient society would be more pressure than she could bear.

When asked if she would take a job working in a store or restaurant, Ruth Ellen replied, "I never really thought about it. It makes me nervous to think about it…scared…I don't know how people will react to me because I am *different*."

For that reason, Ruth Ellen has decided that independent living has enriched her life and her faith in herself.[48]

"I feel good about myself. That's good, isn't it?"

Ruthy on The Phone At Work[49]

---

48   Compliments Steubenville Herald Star
49   Compliments of Ruthy Rodgers

Ruthy would see her mother next at her funeral in 1993. Dorothy Kelps drove her son David and Ruthy to the funeral home. Dorothy, never saying a bad thing about anyone, had nothing good to say about Naomi. She watched Ruthy light up at the only gift, a mug, once sent to her as a Christmas present from Naomi. No visit, no card, no love! This just didn't sit well with the loving Dorothy Kelps. It was at Naomi's funeral that Ruthy's half brother told David, "You take care of my sister." To which David loves to repeat to this day, "I told him, I will, I will!" David said, "I'll beat the pulp out of anyone who hurts Ruthy."

Ruthy's stay with Penny had lasted only two and a half years. But after the independent living move in 1983, Penny was not in Ruthy's life until a recent visit in 2011. Ruthy instantly greeted her with "Penny, Penny!" Ruthy never forgot all that Penny had done for her.

During Penny's 30 year absence, Penny was fighting her own nightmares. She had watched her middle son repeatedly beaten by Bob. She admits that it was at this time that she started drinking. Her drinking accelerated the fights between Bob and herself. The fights were becoming much more physically abusive and her older son would step in to protect her. Penny finally decided to get a divorce after 18 years of marriage. Her ex-husband remarried in three months, confirming all of Penny's suspicions. Her middle son left with her, but her oldest son, Bobby, stayed with his dad to graduate. Her greatest heartache was that her youngest son Mark, age 12, was mad at his mom for the divorce and originally stayed with his dad. Penny worked and went to technical college. After graduating, she got a good job with the Levelor Company, only to have the company move its operations to Mexico.

At the time of the Levelor closing, Penny was involved in a relationship with an alcoholic (now recovered). She took his offer to move in with him since she no longer had a paycheck to pay her own rent. At this time, her son Scott, chose to move in with his Uncle Mike, his dad's brother. Scott's dad had disowned him for leaving with his mom at the time of their divorce.

With no job, Penny was encouraged by former work colleagues and teachers to finish her college degree at West Liberty University. With many special people helping Penny, it was arranged and she completed her BA Degree in three years.

These weren't an easy three years. Her partner tried to discourage her from getting a college education. This put a reminder of dread through every inch of her being. This time Penny followed her own instincts and graduated in May, 1994. In October, 1994, she married the love of her life. With Jerry working at the Wheeling/Pit steel mill coke plant, and her working as a dental hygienist, they made double house payments and rapidly paid off their home on Lake Tappan. Today, Scott is a Deputy Sheriff working in the schools to help children through their transitions. He and Penny share a mutual admiration for their life victories over devastating odds. All three children, now grown, tell her, "Mom, you did good!" They applaud her choice of husband and tease her that she would have to go before Jerry goes in their life!

Penny and Sons [50]

What a wonderful *to date* ending for a beautiful woman who could have taken every excuse used today of victimization. But instead, she chose victory, worked hard and gave hard to make things happen. After she cared for Ruthy, she was called upon to take care of Ruthy's mom,

---

50 Compliments of Penny Smith

Naomi, which she did. She's also entertained her offenders from when she stayed at her aunt's. That takes a forgiving and loving spirit, considering her family had predicted Penny to be a whore and not amount to much. Ruthy's independent life is also victorious today, partially because of Penny's *onward pushing encouragement* for Ruthy to do more with her life. Both have accomplished more than anyone would have ever expected. They are both happy and victorious!!

When Ruthy saw Penny after all the years of separation, she proudly welcomed her into her home where they looked together into Ruthy's family picture albums. They had fond thoughts of Grandma Birdie and Grandpa Arch. But neither wanted to remember or talk about the *middle* of their lives. Penny now had the victory of being an overcomer and Ruthy had hit the *mother load* of families, when she was *adopted* as a Kelps!

Ruthy with Kelps[51]

---

51   Compliments of the Kelps Family

Chapter 8

My "Mudder"

David could often be heard saying, "My mudder." *My mudder* was his stabilizer, encourager, and loved him unconditionally!

David and Dorothy[52]

His mudder, Dorothy Reed Kelps, was the oldest child of Chester and Mary Reed. Chester Reed was a hard working, successful business man who provided well for his family.

Interestingly, my maternal grandfather was my paternal grandfather's (Chester Reed) best friend. They actually both were each other's best man

---

52   Compliments of the Kelps Family

in their respective weddings. To my maternal grandfather, there was no better man than Chester Reed.

Dorothy's mother, Mary, came from a huge German dairy farm family, the Jacob and Barbara Weinman family. I proudly hang this picture on my living room wall of the beautiful family.

Weinman Family[53]

Mary was one of 13 children. The picture shows the nine girls with beautifully coiffed Gibson Girl hairdos and impeccably starched white high collared, ruffled blouses. The three brothers are in their Sunday best suits, with proud Mom and Dad sitting in the center. The fourth son, Charles, had died as a child. A dairy farmer with nine girls – oh my! I knew my grandmother's sisters and sister-in-laws quite well. As all farm families, they worked and played hard. My Grandmother Mary and several other entrepreneurial sisters owned a confectionary store and tea house. Among women in those days, women business owners were a rare breed. Only as I stared at the store picture with my aunt, when I was in my 50's,

53 Compliments of the Kelps Family

did I hear the story of the change in spelling of the Weinman name. The original name had two 'n's at the end of the name. However, when the girls had to pay $.25 per letter to letter the store window, the last 'n' in the name was history!!

Not only did the Weinman sisters work together, once married, they played together every day. No Weinman woman worked, once married. You would never find a speck of dirt in any of their homes and they were all great cooks. Rising early, cleaning their houses and gathering together at a sister's house for lunch and an afternoon of playing the card game, canasta, was their routine. All would scurry home to fix their great dinners by the time their husbands returned from work. These canasta card games had the Weinman rules which allowed the games to continue on, with one being 10,000 in the hole, only to come back and win! My most vivid, horrifying memory of these card fests was the day at three years old when I climbed up behind one of my great aunts on her chair and excitedly cut off her bun hairdo! Lots of noise! I ran quickly downstairs to my mother who was working in my dad's print shop. Clinging like glue and shaking, I relayed the event. To my relieved surprise, she said "Well, if nine grown women can't watch a three year old with a pair of scissors, it is certainly not your fault!" I guess I sat out of a few days of the card playing afternoons in the weeks that followed!

With all of Grandma Reed's siblings, there were lots of cousins for Dorothy to play with daily. Family was always important to Dorothy. There was a complex of family homes in our neighborhood, at the corner of Market Street and Langley (now Rt. 22). Chester Reed had built a home for his bride on Market Street. Then he built another home behind his house on the alley for his widowed mother-in-law, Barbara Weinman. Thus, all the cousins were centered around those two homes because that's where their grandma lived. Years later, Dorothy's brother Harry, would build a home for his family on that corner and a three-story office building that would house his printing business and another business rental. Above the shops, he built two apartments, one for a rental and one for his mother Mary, when Dorothy needed the space of the original family house that she had called "home" as a child. So in this complex of homes, it was a family affair. It was in this circle of homes that David lived until he was 18 years old.

Unfortunately, for all of us on that corner, the Rt 22 highway project took our homes and we thus were scattered.

In the close family dynamics, before Dorothy's married days, she was the anchor for the family business while her brother, Harry, was overseas during World War II. In 1938, Chester Reed had passed away, leaving 21 year old Harry, 23 year old Dorothy, and 13 year old Marty. The letters from Harry to Dorothy during those war years, gives one the realization of her extensive family and business duties.

Mary and Her Two Daughters[54]

---

54 Compliments of the Kelps Family

Mary and Son[55]

June 6, 1943 – Somewhere in Italy

Hello Sis,

There is a little job I want you to do for me. It will only take you a few minutes, so do it now. <u>My address has been changed and I want you to call the folks who write to me with my new address.</u> Now do as I ask now. Our mail is slow and I haven't had any letters from home.

PS Have you done as I asked? You can also Send me some popcorn and a box of cigars.

January 4, 1944 – Somewhere in Italy

To Mother

<u>Sis sent me some writing paper</u> but I can't figure why she sent the kind with "copy" written on it. I can use it to write home but I wouldn't want to send it to anyone else.

---

55 Compliments of the Harry Reed Family

Sis <u>When you had the coupe repainted</u>, you claimed it couldn't be matched and that it was darker. Is it the same color as Ray Sutton's car?

February 8, 1944 – Somewhere in Italy

Hello Sis,

I don't think I have grounds to <u>bawl you out</u> <u>for not writing. I know you have plenty to do.</u> I believe what made you say that was the one letter I sent raising a little heck. I see that it got results. You know when you want something and write for it you can figure it will be two months before you get it. Then I had to write three times to get Jack's address. He could have gone home in that length of time it took to get his address. I went to see him again last Sunday a week ago. We are about 60 miles apart. I'm going to go every chance I get. (Author's note: Jack died in World War II.)

It seems as if the <u>coupe and you have been having your ups and downs</u> or should I say around and around. That car always seemed to handle good for me. It must not know you as well.

You don't need to worry. I did ok for Christmas. I am glad that you also did. Maybe next year we can have a real big one.

It doesn't matter what kind of cigars you can buy. <u>Send me another box</u>. Have you been able to <u>buy any fruitcakes to send</u>. If so send them whenever you can. They go good as an evening snack before we turn in. Now about the <u>National Biscuit Cookies, can you send them? I got the dictionary.</u> I had one that size. <u>I wanted one 5 x 4 x 1" thick</u> like we used in school. They have most of the words in them, this little one is too small.

In your letter you thanked me for the other money order I sent. You are welcome. And if you have anything left, after you deduct <u>the presents you bought for staff</u>, buy yourself something for Valentine's Day. By the way, you never told me <u>what you did at the office for Christmas?</u>

I have learned how to ask for salt and pepper shakers in a couple of different languages. As you can see by the number I sent home what luck I am having buying them. They just don't use things like that in this world. I did send a few home not so long ago.

Glad to know that you have so much outside addressing to do at the office. It will help tie us over. Maybe they will release some material as soon as the war with Germany is over. I sure hope so. That should be finished in the next six months. Just hold out as long as you can.

You know when things look the darkest something always turns up to help us along.

April 24, 1944 Italy

Dear Mother
I see that you are still fixing up our house. The place won't seem the same to me when I get back. I would have been able to help with the work. I know that since I'm away you do a lot of things you shouldn't. Still no letter from Dorothy.
-take care of yourself and don't work too hard.

June, 1944 Italy

Dear Sis –
Mother knows that I sent that money to her so why not have a good time with it.

November 11, 1944 Italy

Dear Sis
I have enclosed a money order for $50.00. This year I'm going to do a little different than last year. I know if I sent the money to mother direct she wouldn't buy something for herself. Now here is what I want you to do. If there's anything you know that mother

would like to have buy it for her. If not enough was sent, let me know and I'll send you more.

I don't know what I put in my letter Oct 6 that made you think I was homesick. There's just times when a fellow gets mad at the way things are going and wishes he was back where he could do as he darn pleases.

Thanks for the information about the office. I want to know what's going on, even if it's bad news. Maybe things will look brighter in the near future. You know how things have been in the past. The darkest hour is just before the dawn.

April 13, 1945

Mother,
I hope you are well and that Martha and her girlfriend get home safely. She sure misses your cooking. She should try some of our meals and then she would appreciate yours that much more. I suppose in another year I will be able to get another of your good meals. Don't take me wrong, I am not homesick but I know the best cook in the world.

June 13, 1945 Falcanaro, Italy

Dear Sis,
I know my birthday is coming up and you will be working to send something. You better skip it. If everything goes as planned we will stay here for three or four months and then return to the States. One thing for sure we are coming home but just how soon is a question. I do feel for sure I'll be home for Christmas. I sure hope so. I don't want four of them away from home.

How are things at the office. From what I have read in the papers, it claims that discharged veterans can buy essential material from the government. If that is so, maybe I can get some material for us when I get home. I think business would be very good if we had the goods to sell.

Since you won't tell my anything about the office I don't know what is going on or what and how to make my plans. You know I won't be a soldier forever. How about taking time out and writing me all about our affairs.

Sis have I in one letter or another said anything that you've taken offense to? Maybe you don't realize it, but you haven't written me a letter this year. I think I asked you in my last letter what was wrong, but received no answers.

On February 8, 1944, Harry wrote from "Somewhere in Italy"

Dear Sis, It seems to me that you have taken a lot more interest in the events of the church. What caused this?

For many, this will be a surprise, to even imagine Dorothy Kelps as a *not involved* church member! For 43 years, Dorothy Kelps would take care of every baby in the nursery of Zion Church. Everyone comes to a decision point in life about their relationship with Christ. When Harry wrote this to his sister, Dorothy, maybe the events of her life took her from church member to a desire to serve Christ. And serve she did. Every Sunday morning, rain or shine, all babies and toddlers were met with the wide smile and warming eyes of Dorothy. She knew her ministry.

As you read Harry's letters, especially towards the end of the war, he seemed rather upset with his faithful, doting sister's non writing. He had written on November 11, 1944:

Dear Sis: In one of your letters you said something about you and Ed going to the show. When did you and him start going places together? Are you trying to hold out on me or was that just a one night affair?

From the first date, Ed and Dorothy were very serious. No wonder brother Harry was put on the back burner – Dorothy was in love. That one night affair lasted through 40 years of marriage, until death do us part, as Ed died in 1986.

Ed and Dorothy[56]

She was in love with their renter, widower Ed Kelps. After Grandma Weinman died, her house on the alley behind Mary Reed's house was rented to Ed Kelps, his wife Anne, and their daughter Margaret Anne. Ed Kelps, as a child, had been raised with his family on Langley. When he married Anne, he was very happy to find a rental in the neighborhood. After years of renting, Ed's young wife became very ill and passed away, leaving her grieving husband with a young daughter to raise. Anne's sister, Kay, moved into the house to co-parent her sister's child.

While Dorothy was enjoying her neighbor during World War II, Harry was clueless of her preoccupation. Of course, he was busy too, being the designated driver for the Generals in Rome. My dad, Harry, chose to smoke as most men did during the war years. He drove a 1935 Indian motorcycle with a radio before he went into the service. His dad wasn't happy with either, so he made him a deal. As long as you don't ever drink alcohol, you can smoke but not in the house. For the motorcycle, Chester took away Harry's keys to the family car. But reluctantly, Chester jumped on Harry's bike one morning when the car wouldn't start. When Harry came home that night, Chester threw Harry the keys but again said,

---

56 Compliments of the Kelps Family

"Never, never, never drink." I suppose there was some reason for Chester's strong convictions, but all I know is that my dad, my brother, myself and my children have carried on that conviction and avoided a lot of life's problems that I have seen happen from the abuse of alcohol.

Harry's 1935 Indian Motorcycle[57]

During the war, Harry's not drinking allowed him to have the benefit of driving privileges for leaving the base. The generals told Harry, "Get us back to the base no matter how drunk we are or how much we protest!" During those nights in Rome, Harry didn't drink, but he gambled enough to win and send funds home to send his younger sister to college, fund the family business and help support his mother. He also carried on his high school yearbook label of *a lady's man*. So he didn't miss the drinking. He had lady friends and knew every card in everyone's hand!

---

57 Compliments of the Harry Reed Family

Rome 1945[58]

Back home, the atmosphere of Dorothy's dating was surrounded with adversity.

Due to Aunt Dorothy's strong faith and Ed's love for Dorothy, it was concluded that they would attend church together at Zion Lutheran. But Aunt Kay insisted that Margaret Ann would go to the Catholic Church with her and be raised a Catholic. Margaret Ann loved Aunty Dorothy, as all did who knew her, so she didn't pay much attention to Aunt Kay's remarks of how Dorothy's pulling Ed from the Catholic Church was causing her dad to be *doomed to hell*. In 1945, a Protestant dating a Catholic was trouble. And Kay was very Catholic.

From the following letters, Dorothy was obviously questioning Ed's love for her while they were dating. She probably needed to be reassured that this widower was ready to love again. She may also have needed his love confessed due to Kay's attitude. Ed's words of love in these letters must have assured Dorothy.

October 9, 1944

Dearest Dorothy:

You asked me for a letter, didn't you. I'll probably see you at least twice or perhaps three times before you get this letter if I am fortunate enough. Last night before I went to sleep I looked up at our moon. I thought then that the

---

58   Compliments of the Harry Reed Family

moon might wane and diminish in size from one month to the other but my love for you will never lessen. It seems strange that it has only been a very short while ago the whole bottom dropped out of my world and everything looked so dark and dreary. You, my dear, have changed all that for me and have made each day worth while looking forward to. In fact when I think of you and our future together, if each day were in a sack and lined up before me I wouldn't be able to wait to see what new happiness there was in each day but would have to run ahead and shake out the contents of each bag as quickly as possible to see what was in store for us. You see my dearest, I always was that way. All I have left of Ann are our child and many precious memories of time we spent together. I know she wouldn't mind my love for you that I have now.

I think I've poured my heart out to you many times in the near past and shall do so many more times in the future.

I was extremely fortunate in knowing and having some one like Ann. We lived for each other without a thought of the rest of the world. To know that feeling again with someone like you is almost too good to be true.

Again I say I love you, my dear and I shall always continue to do so. I hope and pray that your life with me will always be happy as I'm quite sure Ann's was.

I'll be glad when we are married. There will be so many more opportunities to tell you how much I love you. My thoughts are always of you and of our future together. When I'm not able to hold you in my arms I dream of holding you in my arms and whispering in your ear that I love you.

This letter my dear is difficult to write. Don't laugh at it please, because I mean every word that I have written. I've never put my feelings on paper before in my life. But if you wish it my sweetest, I'll put all of my love on record for you to see.

My dear, when you are in my arms and my lips are on yours, I'm really and truly out of this world and transported to a higher plane of happiness than I ever thought could be possible again. Just the sight of you or the sound of your voice thrill me to the core of my being. I feel quite bad right now because it looks as if a whole day may go by without my holding you in your arms and kissing you. When we are married my dear I hope that days like this never happen.

I'll close now. Dear Dorothy with your name on my lips and in my heart.
With all the love that is in me I remain yours forever and a day.

Ed

Mon. Eve. Nov. 13, 1944

Dearest Lover:

I'm here at work now and can't get my mind off you. I just have to write and tell you how much I love you and miss you even if it has only been a few hours since I was with you and less time has passed since I talked to you.

I can't begin to tell you how glad that a love like ours has come into my life to brighten it again. I hope from the bottom of my heart that you feel now and always will, the same way about me. I can not see any thing ahead of us but our mutual love for each other.

Dorothy, my dearest, I can hardly wait for the day to come when we shall belong to each other forever. I could be satisfied to pour my heart out to you every day the rest of our lives. I do hope you realize my deep love for you. I think you do and I'm only sorry I can't do more to prove my love to you than just use words. You are in my heart and mind always, my loved one.

From my mind and my heart I say I love you, I love you, forever and ever.

Ed

Not a dry eye in the place?? For all the romantics, I had to include those letters. Ed truly loved Dorothy and Dorothy truly loved Ed.

Harry was home from the service to walk his sister down the aisle of Zion Lutheran Church. Martha was home from college and mother Mary, with the help of her sisters, had created a lovely wedding for her oldest daughter. If Mary had concerns about Dorothy's marriage to a Catholic, her now having a step-daughter, and the awareness that Aunt Kay had no plans to leave Ed Kelps' home, she never said anything. Her 30 year old daughter was in love, so Mary would celebrate.

Chapter 9

Faith Conflicts

Even though Mary Reed didn't voice any concerns, Ed's former sister-in-law, Kay, was very vocal about Ed going to hell!? She, of course, had to stay in Ed Kelps's home with his bride to make sure her sister Anne's daughter was raised Catholic. Dorothy lived with Aunt Kay's snubs and derogatory thoughts for five years.

In those days, as much as Catholics thought Protestants were going to hell, the Protestant mothers of Steubenville were just as convinced that if your daughter dated a Catholic, she would marry a Catholic who would be an Italian, thus in the mob!!? When my friend stated the latter to me, I agreed. That was exactly what our mothers thought!

Such was the thinking in 1945, as Ed and Dorothy were dating. It took until Vatican II in the 60's for both groups to acknowledge that what was really important was one's belief and confession of Jesus Christ for salvation. I'm not saying that all accepted this truth readily, but ecumenical strides began to take place. My mother, a devoted Methodist, really liked my friend's future husband. They had *liked* each other since age 12 and dated since they were 16. So at age 21, they were ready to marry. One day before they were to be married, while fixing lunch with my mother, she exclaimed, "Do you know her future husband is Catholic?!" Obviously, she had just gotten the word. This was the *shock* of the era of my Mom and Kay. The truth is that being Catholic, Methodist or whatever, isn't going to get you into Heaven. After Vatican II, the Catholic Church preached that we are saved by grace, not works due to the gracious gift of the shed blood of Jesus Christ. Like any gift, it has to be received, regardless of your faith tradition.

Galatians 2:21, written by Paul to the Galatians: "I do not invalidate the Grace of God, for if acquittal from guilt comes through the law, then Christ died to no purpose."

I was aware that even though my friend and her future husband didn't share the same traditions, they shared the same faith. John 5:1, "Everyone who believes that Jesus is the Christ is a born-again child of God." It is best for a common place of worship to be decided prior to marriage due to the importance of a faith based marriage. I knew they had both accepted and confessed Jesus Christ's gift of salvation. My mom knew - one was Protestant – one was Catholic!

Who would have guessed that the reputation of Steubenville would one day be changed due to the world renowned Catholic Franciscan University of Steubenville where people of all faiths would attend? Driving in the parking lot, you will see license plates from every state. When I am greeted in Paris, Rome, Jerusalem, Canada, or Los Angeles, and my Steubenville roots become known, the positive reaction is amazing! It does appear though, that if the world knows of what's happening of great spiritual importance at the University, the city itself is clueless.

Even now, as in the days of Dorothy and Ed's atmosphere of intolerance, you will find the following divisions in Steubenville:

- The Evangelical Catholics *On the Hill*
- The Catholics that want to ignore the university's world wide spiritual effect
- The Protestants that aren't happy with the Catholic's success
- And of course, the total non believers

The meeting of these above sects with total respect could create an interesting economic explosion for Steubenville.

The new *Boom Town* explosion, caused by the industry of fracking, is answered prayer for the City of Steubenville and the University!

(Note in the back of this book, the wise words of Father Mike and the Protestant leaders of Steubenville for an interesting read.)

The University is positioned high on a hill overlooking the Ohio Valley. Many in the city aren't happy with the *Hill* evolution of the city's reputation. Much of this reaction is due to first impressions. In my image business, we teach that one has only 30 seconds to make a good external first impression.

The *first 30 seconds* for the University was not seen as favorable to the citizens of Steubenville. There was a rightful skepticism about the *Hill* due to the over-zealous first graduates of Father Mike's University presidency. Also, many believers from other states came in support of Father Mike's new vision for the failing 200 attendee Catholic College of Steubenville. He had not even wanted this job with a return to Steubenville, but had been appointed with the strong recommendation of a Jewish business owner, Mr. Kobacher, (Payless founder) who sat on the Board of the then small Catholic College. With Father Mike's Harvard law degree, Mr. Kobacher said after the interview, "Well, there is only one choice, Father Mike."

God certainly had plans for Father Mike. God definitely moved His Spirit to alter the college closing. A true spiritual revival occurred. The new evangelical graduates and the supportive new residents created "the community". Like all good things, taken to its extreme, it can become bad. The 1970's had a national movement that didn't spare the University. Christians were being encouraged to be accountable to spiritual leaders. As Father Mike told me, "The problem was that outside groups came into the *community* and designated immature leaders who took the good concept of discipleship and turned it into total authoritarian control." These actions warranted the Bishop to put reasonable activities in place. Not long after this correction, sixty people from the University and city met with the Pope where he gave great accolades to the work of the University.

Father Mike With The Pope[59]

---

59   Compliments of Father Mike Scanlon

As I talked to Father Mike, he shook his head, realizing that the happenings of 40 years ago could still cloud the heads in the people of Steubenville to the point that they can't see what's really happening! I have to agree. In travel, I hear, "Steubenville Franciscan University and its City are awesome." Are all students awesome? No! I am sure some students are sent by their parents to the University in hopes of turning their lives around for good. Therefore, there are bad examples of bad college renters, rowdy bar crowds, and courtrooms of indicted college students which can scar a good reputation. But the statistics show a very small percentage of these actions happening at the Franciscan University compared to other college campuses.

When talking with my friends in the city of Steubenville, today, I share the new world view reputation of Steubenville of which I hear. They are quite surprised! One friend said the truest statement, "I guess while we were down here reeling from the city's decline of the steel mill closings, we missed what was really happening up on the Hill!"

When a city has gone from hookers and gamblers to spiritual recognition, there has been a reputation evolution!

The Kelps courtship and David's growing up years were not in the *spiritual city*, but rather in the city of *gambling and prostitution*. David's aunt had sold her deceased mother's home to a *nice young couple* in a lovely, friendly neighborhood with porches and sidewalks and *good folk*. The phone soon started ringing with neighbor's objections to the new owners, scantily clothed gals and constant traffic of men during all hours of the day and night. The aunt's comments, "Auchdielieber, I left that good Tiffany chandelier for those people!" In Steubenville fashion, the house was next door to the home of a policeman!

On another occasion, an aunt called a dance studio to send a *little dance troupe* into the Methodist church Valentine's party. Imagine the shock of this older congregation watching fifteen 17 year olds who had just come back from Las Vegas! (Steubenville was known for training what Vegas needed – girls, dealers, etc.) The long legs in tight gold shorts came tapping and kicking into the basement of the Methodist church. Odd?? This aunt's comment, "The congregation may ride me out of town on a rail." But no problem, all enjoyed!!?

Truly, Steubenville's reputation has changed! But Aunt Kay could never accept that Ed Kelps should change to be a good Protestant. It made no difference to Kay that the Monsignor had assured 13 year old Margaret Ann that, "It was better to be a good Protestant than a bad Catholic." Don't bother intolerant people with facts.

Chapter 10

FAMILY MATTERS

Dorothy, Ed, Margaret Ann and her Aunt Kay would reside in Grandma Weinman's house, right behind Mary and Chester's homestead.

There was a lot of tension in the *neighborhood*. Dorothy walked into another woman's *home*, even though that home was really Dorothy's own grandmother's home that she had watched her father build! The moving was easy from her mother's home. *Living* was a different story. But complaining and being negative would never be a part of Dorothy Kelps' style. Dorothy was 30 and Ed was 36 when they were married in 1946. Ed had already been a hard working steel worker since 1940. Ed was born in Pittsburgh, Pa. to Episcopalian Lithuanian immigrants. He only finished the eighth grade because his family need him to earn money in order to help the family survive. Both parents had died before Dorothy met Ed.

Ed Kelps [60]

Ed had worked his way up to being a Turn Foreman at the Follansbee Coke Plant of Wheeling Pitt Steel Corporation. By far, it was the worst place to work in the mill. Most called the coke plant the *gates of hell*! But hard working Ed Kelps knew it paid the best and even took the unwanted top paying job by choosing the position of coke plant Turn Foreman. He felt this was more secure for his family's future. The coke plant today in 2011 is the only functioning part of the steel mill, run by seniority older workers. Some have 42 years of service in the mills. Foreman Ed would ride out many strikes, locked in the mill as paid salaried management. These were especially hard times for Dorothy who missed her Ed. Ed would call her several times daily from the mill just to tell her he loved her.

---

60   Compliments of the Kelps Family

Coke Plant[61]

It was my pleasure to find men at the USWA in Steubenville who had worked for Ed Kelps. Carmen Destefano, the finance secretary of the union grievance committee, was sixteen when he worked for Ed who now would be 102 if he were still alive. Carmen led me to others who all shared the same thoughts about Ed's character as a boss. Words were used to describe Ed like *quiet, fair, imposing (6'5" tall), and intimidating.* People said he was untrusting until you proved yourself, and he disliked sluffers. Ed worked for tough bosses, per the men who worked under Ed. One man relayed the story of his first day working at the coke plant with Ed Kelps as his boss. As the new man, he was told to go clean the filthy, dirty, grimy belts of the equipment. That was an awful job. When he went to check on him, Ed found the man sitting, having a cigarette. Of course, Ed *barked* the man to attention and began to chastise the worker. However, as he inspected the work that the new recruit had been asked to do, he was astonished to find that all the work was completed. He immediately apologized to the worker, which was never done by the macho mill men.

---

61 Compliments of Penny Smith

This man said he gained great respect for Mr. Kelps that day, and Ed never again questioned his work. Ed could be tough on a worker who didn't pull his weight. His son, Ron, went into the mill for summer work, to put himself through college. One day when Ron was in the shower room, such a sluffer was complaining about tough Ed. As others tried to quiet the man, telling him that Ron was Ed's son, the man quickly switched to telling Ron how great his father was in the mill. At the dinner table that evening, when Ron relayed the story to his dad, Ed said, "Yea, I catch that guy sleeping on the job all the time!"

Ed worked in the mills for 35 years, retiring in 1975. He saw the good years of the mills. At that time, there were 13,000 employed at Wheeling Pitt Steel. In those years, it was considered unnecessary to go to college. Or if you did go away, after you graduated, you would return to work in the mills due to the high salaries. In 1968, you could make a starting salary of $50,000 per year in the mills. Ultimately you would have 13 weeks vacation, and if you started working at age 16, you would have 30 years in for retirement at the old age of 46. It was a common practice among the families of mill workers to groom their sons to take advantage of generational offerings at the mills. They were like your family. Being part of the union and a worker at the mill was a source of pride and financial success. In the 1950's, you could work at age 16, not go to school and yet still play high school sports. Later, they set the standard that to be hired you had to be a high school graduate.

Ed Kelps wasn't a high school graduate, but he was a loyal, hard working steel man. "Where you working?" was the typical greeting question, meaning where in the mill or on what shift? In the 1980's, the climate changed as foreign cars became the rage and foreign steel became cheaper due to their lack of government regulations. The EPA, per the retired union steel workers, used industry regulation positions to pay back political favors. In the valley, staying with the family became impossible due to job losses. This realization in the 80's broke a lot of hearts – those who left and those who saw them leave. In 2003, the USWA gave up 52% of their wages to try to restore mill jobs. By 2009, all of the steel mills were closed, except the coke plant filled with senior citizens who have seniority.

For Dorothy and Ed, the steel mill was the source of bread and butter and much more. The concept of shift work took Dorothy some getting use to as a new bride. Ed would be by her side in bed at night for three weeks, then gone for three weeks as he worked night turn. There were three eight-hour shifts and the Shift Foreman worked all the shifts at different times. Shift life affected families. Work came first and all plans were made around work.

It wasn't long before Ed and Dorothy shared the exciting moment, as all loving couples do, when the news arrived that, "Yes, you are indeed pregnant!" As all preparations began at that moment, it seemed like just a blink until Dorothy was rushed to the Ohio Valley Hospital to deliver their son, David Allen Kelps, on July 18, 1947. There must have been tense moments at birth, as the umbilical cord was wrapped around David's neck per his caseworker's report. But he was delivered and appeared normal with ten fingers and ten toes. David was welcomed with grand excitement! Dorothy's first child, Ed's first boy, Mary's first grandchild, born on Dorothy's brother Harry's birthday and his middle name, Allen, was named after Ed's brother Al. He was brought home to the loving circle of the family homes, hugs, and lots of love.

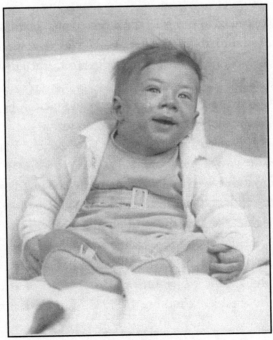

David's Baby Picture[62]

---

62 Compliments of the Kelps Family

As David reached the age of almost two, Dorothy was to deliver her second son, Ron. While Dorothy was at the hospital, David was taken to his aunt's home in the Akron, Ohio area. She noticed some perplexing developmental issues with David. It was noticeable that sitting in his high chair, he was unable to hold his head up. It appeared to her, as a trained teacher, that David's development was not normal. She asked her family physician to make a house call to see David. Only as I was writing this book did our aunt reveal that she had been shocked when the doctor's diagnosis was, "Oh yes, he is definitely retarded and won't live more than a couple of years." She never told her sister of that diagnosis. Simultaneously, Grandma Reed was becoming concerned about David's developmental challenges. She asked Harry's wife, Peg, who also had been a school teacher, if she suspected a problem with David. Peg answered, "There definitely is a problem." Nothing was ever said to Ed and Dorothy about all of these concerns. To quote our 84 year old aunt, "We just didn't talk about those kinds of things back then."

In those days, developmentally disabled children were frequently kept out of sight because of the shame felt by parents. Institutionalization and life long care continued as the generally accepted method for treating those with developmental disabilities. After World War II, several well known celebrities publicly confessed their struggles in raising their developmentally disabled children.[63]

There was first the book in 1950 by Pearl Buck, 'The Child Who Never Grew'. She wrote, "Parents may find comfort in knowing that their developmentally disabled children are not useless, but that their lives, limited as they are, are of great potential value to the human race." Buck's book signaled that there was no longer shame in having a developmentally disabled child. In 1953, Dale Evans wrote 'Angel Unaware' about their mongoloid daughter. Perhaps the most prominent family to deal with the issue of developmental disabilities was the Kennedys. President Kennedy's sister, Rosemary, born in 1918, was diagnosed as mildly retarded. The Kennedy family became major financial supporters of efforts to assist developmentally disabled children. In 1962, Eunice Kennedy Shriver

---

63   Floyd, Barbara L. Editor. *From Institutions to Independence.* Published by the University of Toledo Press

started a special camp for the developmentally disabled. People started thinking about the subject.[64]

Even though times and thoughts were changing concerning the care and acceptance of having a developmentally disabled person in your family, it was wasted on Ed and Dorothy Kelps because to them, David was to be treated the same as a normal child. Because to them, he was.

It would not be until David had failed kindergarten twice that Ed and Dorothy heard the word *retarded* used to describe their oldest son.

David's Kindergarten (second row far right)[65]

By the time David needed to be taken to special education classes in the public school downtown, there would be four other Kelps children. With Ed and Dorothy being older when married, these children came close together. There was Ron (former Vice President of Goodyear, Singapore), Kathy Pavlik (Special Education and Gifted Children's teacher), Ken (Pharmacist), and Beverly Lipinsky (with crippling adult multiple sclerosis and mother of seven children). Of course, there was also Margaret Ann who was married at age twenty to a Washington, DC lawyer. Not bad for a father with an eighth grade education!

---

64 Floyd, Barbara L. Editor. *From Institutions to Independence.* Published by the University of Toledo Press
65 Compliments of the Kelps Family

Sibling Family Picture[66]
Front Row: Beverly Kelps Lipinsky, Back Row: Ken,
David and Ron Kelps, Kathy Kelps Pavlik

Kathy relayed to me that her mother (Dorothy) was afraid to tell Grandma (Mary) about her pregnancies after she had three children. Mary's reasoning was, "You have a healthy boy, healthy girl, and one retarded child." Dorothy had her hands full! But if God made anyone to be a mother, it was Dorothy Kelps. As all the kids on Langley Avenue would agree, Dorothy Kelps was the neighborhood mom. Ron's best friend has tears in his eyes to this day, when he tells how welcomed Dorothy would make him feel when he knocked on the door at 2:00 am because he had just been kicked out of his house by his drunken father. Never did Dorothy just have her family to feed, but rather all of us in the neighborhood loved to eat at the Kelps' table. It could be just bags of fresh bread with honey

---

66 Compliments of Ruthy Rodgers

or toast with butter and brown sugar, but there was a happy spirit always present. And there was milk, lots of milk. The Kelps family went through eight gallons of milk each week! Ed once told his rifle shooting buddies that he had to give up shooting because he had *milk disease.* With their shocked looks, he continued, "A large milk bill every week."

The Kelps family had two loving parents. A mom that was a true mother with the difficult job of keeping five children quiet in the day when her husband worked the night shift. Ed was a dad who worked hard to provide. He also played with his children, providing lots of recreational outlets.

We have certainly seen a lot of dysfunctional family life, immoral consequences, etc. so far in this book. It is my pleasure to now show you the Kelps family that *works!* With much prayer and planning, loving and caring vision, this family created the independence, contentment and happiness, not just for David, but also for Ruthy.

Chapter 11

THE CHARACTERISTICS OF A LOVING FAMILY

The greatest compliment that can be paid to parents from grown children has got to be, "I wish I could be more like them." I heard this repeatedly, in asking the Kelps children for evaluations of their mother and father. You will be able to agree when you note below, the opinions of Ed and Dorothy as listed by their children.

Our mother Dorothy:
- Strong woman
- Strong belief – only read her bible and newspaper
- Ministered through the church nursery for 43 years
- Never met a kid she didn't like
- Couldn't see the bad in anyone
- Fed homeless bums who came to their door
- Motherly
- Kind
- Patient
- Good friend to friends

Probably the best way to explain Dorothy Kelps' character is to quote her son-in-law, Al Pavlik, who gave up his living room to Dorothy during her invalid state in her last few years, "I wouldn't do that for anyone else but Dorothy Kelps!"

Describing our father, Ed:
- Good Man
- Loving
- Consistent

- Played by the rules
- Assured his wife of his love daily
- Checked in at home regularly during work
- Religious
- Took good care of Davey
- Spent non-work time with family
- Hard worker
- Smart
- Man of many interests
- Giving to his family
- Family Man
- Devoted to Marriage

To best describe *Big Ed's* family devotion is to tell of his tears shed when he told Dorothy, "A ferris wheel broke at the fair. That could have been our children." Or to tell you how he excitedly would bring cheesecake home to the family on the first Sunday of the month after he was paid. Or to tell of his okaying the dance held for the neighborhood kids in his backyard right after he had planted grass. Or to tell you of the day he walked from his home in Steubenville, Ohio, to work at the coke plant in Follansbee, West Virginia, because his daughter Beverly needed the car!

Per their daughter, Kathy Kelps Pavlik, "It is really funny when I look back at our childhoods. For some reason (who knows why), I thought we were really well off. I knew nothing about money. But I knew that we had plenty to eat (for sure with my mom cooking!!). We had at least the same amount of new clothes as any one else in the neighborhood and more than some. We went on vacation every year (even if it was to my sister's…what better place to visit than DC??? – I still love it!). We had family around that we thought were great…best friends ever!… I always felt that my life was (and is) really good. Church and youth group were a wonderful part of that. If life wasn't good…I sure wasn't aware at all."

As we further define the atmosphere, attitudes and actions of the home that raised David Kelps and gave unconditionally to Ruthy, we will see the family *secrets* that allowed David and Ruthy to have the ability to live independently.

Proverbs 29:15, "A child left to himself brings shame to his mother."

With all the love in the Kelps family, there was also the *wooden spoon* and an occasional threat of *the belt*; David included. In David's own words, "My father loved me a lot. He would take me fishing all the time. But if I needed it, he would get the belt out and whoop me!" David then agrees that this was probably a good thing since it taught him that he had to follow the rules and restrain his temper.

Even loving Dorothy had the children's respect as she had the powerful *wooden spoon*. Beverly Kelps says she probably *tested* the spoon the most. When she was sent to make her bed, she crawled out the window – only once, due to the *spoon*. Kathy Kelps watched Bev's testing and knew it was coming when Bev complained about the toast style that Dorothy had just given her. As Dorothy turned her back on Bev, Bev thought she was free to put her toast above her lip and stick out her tongue. Kathy remembers gasping at this bad judgment and watched as Dorothy turned around in time to see this act of disrespect. The *spoon* was drawn from the drawer and Bev learned a lot about respect in just a few moments!

These corrective moves were a great lesson in cause and effect. No discipline in the Kelps home was done to abuse the child, but rather to prepare them for society.

Much of the behavioral medication distributed in schools today has accelerated from a small box to drawers of pills. I am not a professional or psychologist, but I wonder if the use of pills for behavioral modification hasn't contributed to the drug use to alter one's mind. The definition of abuse and discipline has become so distorted that we now may have raised generations who weren't taught to be responsible adults, mothers, fathers, wives, and husbands. Maybe the pills have replaced the spoon??

I shudder at the thought of abused children who are beat senselessly by unloving parents. But I also shudder at children who aren't disciplined or taught to become responsible citizens and family members, and who don't understand cause and effect.

As Kathy says, "There were fair rules, you knew them, and you asked for a spanking if you disobeyed the rules." It must have worked because Dorothy's five children are still happily married with over 25 years of marriage each. That is quite a record in today's world.

Kelps Siblings and Mates[67]
(Niece's Wedding)

There was much heartache that Dorothy experienced while raising David, but the family only remembers her getting mad at David, when as a small child, he would get so busy playing outside that he would not take time to come in to go to the bathroom. Bev remembers her mother upset and saying, "He sheet his pants again." Not a swear word, but close!!

Never would there be swearing around Dorothy Kelps. Once Kathy referred to a college roommate as a *bitch* at the dinner table and Bev gasped. Bev only remembers one time that she heard her Dad swear in anger. Bev said she actually was scared when that occurred. You just didn't hear that in the Kelps' home. I am not saying that it didn't get picked up later, but the children did not hear any foul language at home.

Church was a non-option in the Kelps' home. You never even thought about a different option for Sunday morning. And it wasn't just church, it was Sunday School and Church. The entire family would attend, including Ed. Kathy remembers a time when Ron first got his mill summer job and

---

67   Compliments Kathleen Davidson

had to miss Sunday church. Kathy thought this was sacrilegious!! Ron, like his mom and dad, was a hard worker. He actually worked at two different mills in the summer for his college funds. This work was sixteen hour days plus an hour of drive time added to each day. No one did that in those terrible mill conditions. In those summers, if Ron wasn't working, he was sleeping! But his work habits created a nice life for his family. I am sure that Ron, like all of us in the circle of family houses, knew life wasn't easy – just worth the effort.

Can you imagine Dorothy and Ed's dilemma of raising five children plus the *neighborhood*, with shift work and daytime sleeping! All the kids remember the door swinging shut and banging right outside Ed's bedroom. The children also remember that it took until the third week of night shift for *Grumpy* to set in.

But when Ed wasn't working night turn, the Kelps family played together. When David was a child, the Kelps would take picnics to Sportsman Park. The Sportsman Park was good for David. This was a place where he was in a controlled play area as he fished with his dad, swam in the lake with his brothers and sisters, or learned to shoot a bow and arrow in a safe environment. Also, there was the great picnic food that Dorothy could throw together in five minutes when Ed said, "Let's go!"

David With Bow and Arrow[68]

---

68   Compliments of the Kelps Family

On A Picnic[69]

Dorothy and Ed provided a sheltered, independent attitude concerning David. He was never left at home alone or thought as a burden to his siblings. To quote his sister, Kathy, "It is kind of funny looking back...it is just the way it was. None of us thought anything was unusual, it is just what our life was. We really didn't think we were different from any other family...if anything...we thought our life was better. We had parents who loved us, and we had siblings, cousins, aunts, and uncles who looked out for us and made our lives good, and we thought that was the way everyone lived...or should."

Once it was determined that David would attend special education classes at Grant Jr. High, Dorothy concluded that there would be no bus

---

69 Compliments of the Kelps Family

or lunchtime for David where he could get into trouble. As Dorothy's early morning routine, there would be four children to ready for the school across the street, plus she would drive David several miles to his downtown school. A few hours later, it would be her job to pick up David at his school and bring him home to eat lunch with his siblings around the family kitchen table. Then the drive back to school as Dorothy drove David down the hill, only to pick him up again at the end of his school day! Dorothy knew that David's temper and large size might someday get him into trouble, as kids taunted and teased him. So there was no price too large to pay to keep her beloved David out of trouble. At this age, it would be possible, but might not always be possible as he got older. He was a strong and a very large child. Most of his behavioral problems were due to his temper. Since he was often teased, I am sure Dorothy's heart broke as David ran into the house with tears streaming down his cheeks. His mom was always his refuge from the moment when kids teased or tormented him, or when he got into trouble for using his strength in dangerous ways. Often, his misunderstandings created frustrations which led to anger that many times spilled over into violence. It had to be hurtful to see your child tearful after school from verbal abuse, and yet not going to school was not an option for any child in the Kelps family. When I asked David's sister Kathy if David got into trouble at school, she replied, "I don't remember David causing trouble in school, like my parents would accept anything else."

In the *family circle of homes*, David was sheltered. Most any day you could find many grandchildren playing cards at Grandma Reed's home. We were a family of card players and even at the young age of two, Grandma thought you could start learning canasta. But for David's daily visits, he still remembers Grandma's wonderful soft sugar cookies and hard tack candy called *bullets* (brown sugar and peppermint) that were always readily available in her refrigerator. The Reed family genes allowed for trim, thin bodies in our childhood, miraculously amongst the butter, candy and sweets that flowed non-stop at the Reed and Kelps homes.

David's freedom also extended to the neighborhood. He was still conquering his tricycle at age eight. It was a large tricycle and so was its rider!

David and His Tricycle[70]

He would develop at Grant School, the nickname *Turkey*. It was appropriate because of his long neck. So in the neighborhood and town, he was known as *Turkey*. But to his family, he was *Davey*.

When Davey came home from school one day, he asked his mother for lard. "Lard?" she said, "What for?" David wanted it because the black kids in his school used it and he wanted to try it so he could have curly hair! Another funny misjudgment happened when David and his family (all seven of them) went to visit their married sister in her one bedroom home in Washington, D.C. They were having a picnic in the backyard – I'm sure to get everyone outside. When David saw a bee on his new brother-in-law's head, he decided the large board leaning against the house would work just fine to *smack* the bee and of course his brother-in-law's head! Ouch!!

It wasn't intentional, but David also got the *raw end of the deal* often during neighborhood pranks. The family and neighborhood kids still laugh at the snowball story.

The Kelps home on Market Street was next to the road going to the downtown area. So, during a snowy *school closed day*, all the neighborhood

---

70   Compliments of the Kelps Family

kids met on the Kelps's front lawn to hurl snowballs at passing cars. It was all in fun until David hit a driver's windshield. Oh boy! As the driver slammed on his breaks and started to get out of his car, everyone scattered except David, who was still rejoicing at his bull's-eye shot! The driver jumped out of his car, grabbed David, and sped off! As the other kids peered around the corner, their eyes were huge and their screams were very loud! The neighborhood gang went charging into Ed's bedroom where he had just gone to sleep from working the midnight turn shift. There was no quiet entry into his bedroom. Ed abruptly awoke to everyone shouting, "Davey's been kidnapped!!" Ed immediately went into a raging action plan. He pulled on his clothes and went storming out the front door. As he flew to get to his car, he was stopped by a police cruiser in his driveway with sirens blaring and a grinning David in the back seat! As soon as Ed went charging to the policeman in the car, the officer immediately rolled up his window to talk with Ed through a one inch opening. Ed was like a *father bear* charging to protect his cub. Right before the policeman locked the doors, David jumped out! Ed was yelling, "Where's the guy who kidnapped my son?!" David was yelling even louder to the crowd of family and neighbors, as his tearful mother hugged him. "Wow, I got to ride in the cop car with the sirens!" shouted David. The officer backed out of the drive as fast as he could while all the attention turned to David! For Ed, falling back to sleep wasn't so easy!

Snowball Day[71]

---

71   Compliments of the Kelps Family

One day when Ed was working the afternoon shift, he came home to the family excitement that Ron Kelps had cornered a rat in the kitchen. Apparently the rat came in during the new kitchen remodeling. As Ron had the broom, swinging fiercely at the rat in sheer fear, Ed entered the *game* to help corner the rodent. The only problem being that in Ron's fear, he was wildly swinging the broom hitting Ed and missing the rat! Ed finally declared, "Get the darn rat, not me!!" Kathy remembers she and her mom rolling on the floor with laughter during this mill homecoming!

After David had conquered his two-wheel bike and the training wheels were removed, his world of independence was opened widely. At this point, he had a few neighborhood friends who didn't have cars and would ride all over the county with David. Early one morning as Ed was getting up to go to work on the day shift at the mill, he found Dorothy in tears exclaiming that David hadn't come home. Ed jumped in the car at 4:00 am and started searching for David. David says it was about 5:30 am when his dad spotted him at Collier's Way, West Va., and drug him and the bike home before Ed went to work that morning.

It was probably at this time that Ed decided to set up CB radio equipment for David in his third floor bedroom. David could now communicate with the world through his CB handle, *Turkey*. Realizing David's interest, Ed would take him to meetings and get-togethers with the Steel Valley Crusader CB friends in nearby towns. *Redman* was a good CB buddy to David. *Redman* and his wife, *Chevy Lady*, would have all his CB friends come to enjoy his farm on the hill near Costonia, a few miles outside of Steubenville. David and his father often went there just to fish or enjoy the view of the rolling hills, and to enjoy *Redman's* family.

In David's later teen years, he had been kicked out of the city swimming pool which was just down the street from their home. His crime, doing cannonballs to douse the lifeguard! Fun for David, but can you imagine 7 ft and 330 lbs of water displacement!!! But David took this ousting as a good reason to ride his bike with his friends out into the country to a swimming hole they all loved with a swing rope at Lake Lodge. David would ride his bike for miles, even 25 miles out past Carrolton, Ohio. Being on his bike gave him independence. His determination to conquer his bike over several years proved to be worth the scrapes, the sneers, and the frustration.

Conquering the Two Wheeler[72]

Ed found that Dorothy and David could relax at Sportman's Lake. So for his family he bought a school bus that had been converted into a camper by Dorothy's brother Harry. Through several mill strikes, Dorothy and the family camped for the summer.

The Kelps Camper[73]

---

72 Compliments of the Kelps Family
73 Compliments of the Harry Reed Family

Living on Langley Street also meant Friday night Big Red football was right at the end of the street. Who needed a ticket when the neighborhood gang could see it all through the fence in the alley behind Langley homes. Football fever on Friday night in the fall was certainly part of the neighborhood!

As David watched the football games, he was mostly excited about the end zone scoreboard blazing with fire from the horse's mouth with every touchdown! Winning is important in Steubenville. Long before the legal lottery, there were *numbers* to be played in Steubenville. Football, of course, being one form of potential wins. Only lately as I was talking to a Steubenville resident did I share my conservative husband's experience with the Steubenville *numbers*. We were married on 6-27-70. Much to the excitement of our tuxedo tailor, Scott's tux was the same number, 62770. Well, this was too much for the tailor to ignore! Scott had no idea what he was talking about and came back to the church with the story of the crazy tailor trying to get him to play the *numbers*. As I was relaying the story, a grin came upon my Steubenville friend's face. I got married the same day here in Steubenville and I've played that same number for 42 years! Of course, I asked, "Have you won or lost?" to which he smiled and said, "I've won more than I've lost."

My mom remembers the good-looking Italian Dino Crocetti (Dean Martin), her class member, sitting in the cigar store window as he waited to be called to run the numbers for the mob.

There was a blue law that forbade stage shows in Pittsburgh on Sundays. Big acts that played in Pittsburgh would cross the river and perform on the Lord's Day at the Capitol Theater in Steubenville. One day after performing, Glen Miller went upstairs in the theater to the ballroom and heard Dean singing with Al Arter's group. Somebody asked Miller what he thought of the music. Archie Crocetti would never forget Miller's response, "Well the music is pretty good, but that singer will never make it."[74] Now there was a bad prediction!

Dean's family came to Steubenville to work in the steel mills. They worked, they slept, they ate, living together with other laborers from the old country in the Italian community known as the *piccolo abruzzo*. They took care of their own and they prevailed.[75]

---

74 "Dino", Author Nick Tosches
75 "Dino", Author Nick Tosches

My mom remembers another night at the Capitol Theater when all of her friends gathered to see their good friend clean up on the talent show. That was, until they heard the good looking Italian, Dino, start to sing. Of course, the rest is history. There is still a Dean Martin Day in town, where his daughter comes to sing in a small bar with an "interesting" history. Of course, this is the city where the largest gambling dealer's father dies and all the judges come to the funeral and hug his neck?! The biography "Dino" by Nick Tosches sets aside 186 pages to develop the Steubenville, Ohio atmosphere. It is very interesting.

Thank goodness during David's young years the gutter culture didn't include drugs. As I graduated from high school in 1968, most of us agree that at that time, we knew of only one person on drugs. I am not saying there weren't more, but it wasn't the common topic of conversation that it is today. I remember watching the Godfather movie and watching the older mob leaders being deadset against handling drugs. Obviously, these guys had other vices. But it was the younger generation, like in the movie, that brought drugs into the community. The youth of America, the city of Steubenville, and the lives of the Godfather's grandchildren have been largely destroyed due to drugs.

Fortunately, David will declare, "No, I never used drugs." and he has been convinced along that way that only *stupid people* use drugs.

Steubenville may not have had the best of atmospheres to raise successful children, but there are many families like the Kelps family who succeeded in spite of the interesting culture.

Dorothy and Ed Kelps believed in all their children, including David. They loved their children, disciplined their children, and prepared them for life by example. This life was not void of challenges or pain.

Such was the midnight moment when Dorothy heard the knock at the door.

Chapter 12

APPLECREEK

"Yes officer, can I help you?" Dorothy asked wrapping her robe tightly around her thin waist.

"Is this the home of David Kelps?" the officer asked. Dorothy responded, "Yes, I'm his mother."

"Please get him ma'am, we need to talk to him."

As Dorothy went to get David, she rousted Ed and said, "Something's wrong. The police are here and they want to speak with David."

As the three descended the stairs and entered the living room, Ed Kelps wanted to know what this was all about. The officer started with words that every mother dreads: "Well Sir, we have to take David in for questioning. He's been accused of attempting to climb into a neighbor's daughter's third floor bedroom window."

This was 1967 and David was twenty years old. As David started repeatedly confessing his innocence, Ed demanded more information. At this point in time, the family was no longer in the security of the *family circle of homes*. This incident occurred after Dorothy had to abandon her family home of 48 years due to the Rt. 22 highway project. No longer was David sheltered with family and the *Langley* neighborhood that watched over everyone.

The officer explained, "The neighbor says that he heard noise outside his house and when he went to investigate the situation, there was a ladder leaning against the house to his daughter's bedroom. All he saw was a tall frame darting away. The daughter claims it was David and the parents are pressing charges."

Dorothy immediately turned to David and said, "Davey, did you do this?" There was never a question that David would tell her the truth. Since he could talk, he would tattle on himself and never disguise his behavior.

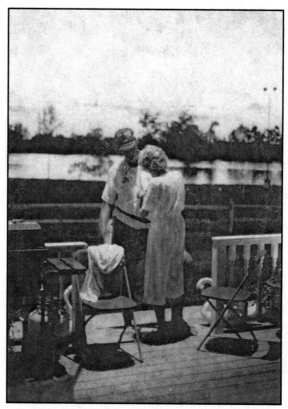

David and His Mother Were Very Close[76]

David adamantly said, "No Mudder, I didn't, I didn't." For Dorothy and Ed that was enough, but for the officer, the charges would still hold.

The next few weeks were scary as they hired a lawyer for $1,000.00, (1968, $,1000.00) which was a lot of money for this mill family. They watched David be incarcerated and had many sessions in the judge's chambers. It was concluded by the authorities that there would be no court case, but rather David would be sent to a facility called *Applecreek*.

Dorothy's heart sunk, but she had no other choice than to accept this verdict. As David was led off to Applecreek, Beverly Kelps described the scene as, "Awful, just awful!" David was reassured by his family that they

---

76 Compliments of the Kelps Family

would visit often and that promise was never broken. Families ill equipped or unwilling to deal with a disabled loved one frequently dropped them off at Applecreek. About fifty percent of those families never returned. Most residents were there by court orders and doctor referrals.

The sites and sounds of David's new home are documented from an article from the Columbus Dispatch by Alan Johnson during the time of David's stay.

Dorothy and Ed left David in 1968 in a facility for the mentally retarded, developmentally disabled, feeble minded, mentally ill, alcoholics, cerebral palsy victims, unwed mothers, and others who just didn't *fit into society*. For decades, conditions in Ohio institutions such as Applecreek were deplorable.

Barbara Jones who worked at Applecreek as a speech pathologist recalled her early impressions of Applecreek. "There was a large room of probably 90 to 100 adult size cribs and there were people with varying degrees of disabilities that lay in cribs all day long." She stated this for an audio documentary, 'Lest We Forget,' by a Dayton disabilities advocacy organization. Jones said, "I saw row after row after row of people just staring at the ceiling or staring off to the side. Some folks could only stare in the position in which they were left because they didn't have the ability to move their own bodies."[77]

Claire Alexander, age 82, said, "Applecreek was a hell hole in 1970 when he took his son John there. There was a mixture of wild kids running all over the place. The doors were kept shut, like going to a prison."

John Kolarovsky, another worker at Applecreek, said "The rooms had bare walls and no furniture other than a bed and dresser. There was a 'timeout room' for unruly patients – a bare eight foot by ten foot room with mesh on the window and a two-inch thick locked steel door. It wasn't a nice place."[78]

David hated the long, dark, narrow halls of Applecreek. He did receive a few extra privileges, probably for three reasons: 1) David wasn't mentally ill; 2) David would outsmart nurses who administered the medicine by putting it under his tongue and then spitting it out when they left. He did this because he said, "With the pills I couldn't think or be me." And, 3) David had visitors, lots of visitors.

---

77 "Home No More", by Alan Johnson, The Columbus Dispatch, Columbus, Ohio
78 "Home No More", by Alan Johnson, The Columbus Dispatch, Columbus, Ohio

Kathy remembers going to visit David on weekends from Kent State University. She was impressed that they had created a bed for him, by cutting two beds and welding them together. She remembers thinking he didn't have that at home as his feet would hang way over in his regular bed.

David's parents visited three times per week, assuring themselves that he was surviving in conditions where suffering and abuse were alleged. They were rightfully concerned about his initial reports of having diarrhea as he tried to become accustomed to institutional food versus the cuisine of Dorothy Kelps. He also reported being hosed down, and lack of freedom. I'm sure these visits kept David from much more abuse.

His sister, Beverly, remembers making a visit to David with her strapping, large football player boyfriend from Ohio Northern University. They had taken a weekend trip to see Davey. This was Jim Lipinski's first sighting of David or the institution. As Bev ran to David with the excitement of seeing her brother, she totally forgot *Lip* for a few minutes. As she turned to introduce Lip to David, she saw Lip as white as a sheet, scared and surrounded by hundreds of Applecreek's residents gawking at this big man. When David saw the situation, he declared, "Break it up! Break it up!!" Everyone scattered and Jim started breathing normal again! Jim would become the very unselfish, loving husband to Bev (who unfortunately was diagnosed later with multiple sclerosis), and he became the favored brother-in-law who often entertained Davey.

Yes, David had visitors and the other *residents* would surround the family. Everyone so wanted attention, but never had visitors – sometimes for a lifetime. It was reported in the Columbus Dispatch article by Alan Johnson that the doctors recommended to one set of parents who placed a child at Applecreek, "Forget you have got her, place her, she's not going to live more than a year anyway."[79] She outlived her doctor's prediction by 53 years. Even the resident doctors were impressed that the family came to visit David so often. Even on brother Ron's summers of working two shifts at the mill, his friend remembers driving to Applecreek with Ron to see David. These trips were two hours each way.

No one in the family is sure, but everyone thinks that during the time of David's stay at Applecreek, eugenics was a common practice. Eugenics

79 "Home No More", by Alan Johnson, The Columbus Dispatch, Columbus, Ohio

is forced sterilization. Originally it was used because at the turn of the century mental retardation was thought to be hereditary. Records now prove that mental illness is inherited, but not mental retardation. But this practice started to fall out of favor by 1930, yet did not end until 1981. The concern is that people with disabilities could be marginalized if society begins to select children based on sex, appearance, intelligence, and the absence of birth defects. Of course, Hitler did this during World War II to make the *perfect race*. China still does this to allow only one child to be born to a family, and America has chosen the tool of abortion to eliminate unwanted lives. And of course, euthanasia is looming on the forefront stage of the *useless* elderly. All of the above are concerning?

For whatever experiences David had at Applecreek, he will not talk about any of his time there. He will shake his head when asked if he has comments and says, "No I don't – uh, uh, not good place to me, it was like bad." This from a man who could talk your leg off about every experience he has had since birth!

Oh by the way, did I tell you that years later, David's accuser confessed that it was her boyfriend, not David who had been in her bedroom that night! Dorothy never doubted David! All of those years at Applecreek were unnecessary!

During David's six year stay, there was an uprising by parents for better care. Many journalists picked up on these stories and parent lawsuits against the state began. It was because of those articles, parents, and lawsuits that the care of developmentally disabled children was returned to the local level, with public schools and non-profit organizations providing services. However, the question of how to care for these adults who outlive their parents has become an issue. In 1960, Dr. Raymond Horn chaired a committee to see how Ohio could improve its care facilities. It was recommended that there be a county system to oversee programs for developmentally disabled persons funded by local, state, and federal funds. This legislation was passed and approved in 1967; the state school started being replaced with county programs and educational facilities.[80]

Again, I never pass up the opportunity to champion and vote for funds to be allocated to the developmentally disabled. As I had a tour of

---

80 "Floyd, Barbara L. Editor. *From Institutions to Independence*. Published by the University of Toledo Press

the new juvenile jail facility in our county, I was perplexed as to why there are more funds to make these luxurious facilities for juvenile offenders to workout, bulk up, and re-enter once they are released versus providing funds for the developmentally disabled. One parent of an Applecreek resident proclaimed, "The State of Ohio takes better care of a murderer than a handicapped child." He said this when Governor Robert Taft decided in 2003 to close several facilities for the developmentally disabled to save the state 23 million dollars per year.[81]

I am totally reminded as we talk about institutions that we may have *thrown the baby out with the bathwater.* The dangers to families raising children, the cost to businesses, the fear of the elderly, and the too frequent occasions of rape, make me realize that we have become terrorized and held hostage in our country by the mental illnesses of drug crazed or unsupervised developmentally disabled persons. Our jails are overcrowded, when what may be needed is more totally supervised, clean, moral hospital dynamics with medical staff working alongside wardens. When we think of the daily happenings of child abduction, etc., we need to conclude that no one in their right mind does this. Those people need clinical shelter, with no hope of returning to the public sector. For some there is no other choice, but for David, he was released to his wonderful family and to the best years of his life! David had survived another hurdle in his young life of 27 years. David's story is about the incredible triumph of the human spirit over unfathomable adversity, courage over fear, dignity over disgrace.

David was resilient, just as his family's example had taught him. During the 60's, Dorothy would have to move from her family homestead, lose her mother to leukemia, lose the family/neighborhood protection for David, watch her falsely accused son be sent to Applecreek, and see her step-daughter die at a young age. She also sent three children off to college at Kent State University leaving only one child Ken at home, and she saw her husband suffer a heart attack. Of course, a woman's age of 44 to 54 is an interesting *phase* all by itself!! But I never saw Dorothy be anything but positive or smiling during those difficult times. I do remember her sitting in her home, alone one night, reading the Bible when I stopped by to see her. I also remember a conversation with her about her friend's husband losing his job. The friend had told Dorothy that she was having

---

81   "Home No More", by Alan Johnson, The Columbus Dispatch, Columbus, Ohio

trouble with depression. Aunt Dorothy told me, "All these years, I thought how nice it must be for her to have a husband that didn't work shifts, had all weekends off, had a clean home where everything fit and there was a separate bedroom for each of her children . But I now really think my life has been wonderful even without those things." I suppose it was the reflection of the sometime chaotic household that may have given occasion to those previous thoughts. But at the bottom of it all, Dorothy was above everything in spirit.

So now it was 1974 and a weak David, for whatever reason unknown to us who are still alive, would come home.

The Family and a Weak David at the Time of His Return from Applecreek[82]

Chapter 13
WHAT WOULD DAVID DO NOW

One thing was for sure, Ed Kelps would find a means by which David could become productive in life. "Idle hands are the devil's workshop." That was an obvious belief in the Kelps household. There was no way that Ed was going to let David lay around the house.

David had always worked from the time he left Grant School at fifteen years of age in 1962. David had gotten 1000 hours of training from the Mahoning Valley Vocational School in Vienna, Ohio. This program was with the State of Ohio Department of Vocational Division through the Ohio Department of Health, Education and Welfare. He earned this certificate in March of 1965. It was for the completion of the custodial course. He also trained at the Goodwill Industries. It was at this job that he successfully conquered on his first day, the sorting of nails, screws, etc. However, when the bell range announcing the end of the day, he realized he could go home. He exclaimed, "Good, I didn't like this job anyway!" He proceeded to mix all of his day's sorting together into a pile.

He was assigned a job through supportive employment to work at the city water department. This was a job subsidized by the State of Ohio for those who completed the state work training program. Even though David's strength allowed him to turn those water valves with a fraction of the time needed by the other employees, there was a lot of angst towards him because he was paid as much as other workers. This was due to his salary being subsidized by state funds for hiring developmentally disabled workers. His salary didn't sit well with the other city workers who were unaware that it was subsidized by the state. They just knew this developmentally disabled employee made as much each week as they were making.

There was a bar/pool hall around the corner from David's home. David would stop in after work with his fellow workers. The bartender always watched out for David and wouldn't give him more than two beers. For some reason, one evening a particular worker had concluded that he was going to antagonize David. He made sure David had drunk seven beers given to him that night, before he started to poke him in the chest, backing David up against the wall. In the words of David, "I rebelled and scared the bee-jeebers out of this guy!" David picked the man up by the shirt and proceeded to shove him against the wall. The man had a split second vision that David could kill him. He begged off and David dropped him. But that was all that was needed to happen for David to get fired the next day. It was reported that he was *Dangerous!* As David relayed to his sisters that his father then became his *drinking buddy*, both responded simultaneously, "No way!" Neither had seen their father ever have a drink nor had they heard of him drinking. We all surmised that this was just one more step in Ed's sheltering of David's independence. He would go with David where he might get into trouble.

But David was not happy with this firing. So in the next week, he approached a city councilman with his insistence that he had bills to pay and needed a job. He was soon to be hired on the city street cleaning crew and worked there for two years.

It wasn't until 1979 that David found his career at Jeffco Workshop. I can't praise this organization enough for the exceptional work they do. Hopefully, the people of Jefferson County will continue to purchase the products produced by Jeffco and support this workshop which gives developmentally disabled people a sheltered work environment with the respect of earning a wage.

JeffCo Contest Winner[83]

The way in which the American society has treated people with developmental disabilities has come full circle. In the colonial era, they were cared for by their families in their communities, and were generally not an object of scorn or fear like those who were mentally ill. Although they were often labeled as the *village idiot.*

By the 1850's, Americans began to believe that the best way to treat such people was to institutionalize them, outside of their communities and away from others.[84]

These early institutions emphasized education. Sequin of France promoted the *physiological education theory* that developmentally disabled people could be educated by exciting their will and training their senses. Thus they could become socialized.[85] The Kelps certainly fostered David's will to be socialized. David would never be shy! Just like the early institutions focused on teaching vocational skills, the Kelps family was determined to have David trained, and certainly there would be no one

---

83   Compliments of Ruthy Rodgers from the Steubenville Herald Star
84   Floyd, Barbara L. Editor. *From Institutions to Independence.* Published by the University of Toledo Press
85   Floyd, Barbara L. Editor. *From Institutions to Independence.* Published by the University of Toledo Press

idle in the Kelps household. The Sequin theory had a goal to keep feeble minded youths from becoming feeble adults.[86]

It became obvious that there were two groups of developmentally disabled persons: those who were trainable and those who weren't. Long term custodial care became the norm.

Institutions continued to struggle with education versus custodial care by those who took their message to the state legislature for better conditions for the mentally disabled. One person in the legislature is quoted as saying, "Nothing in human form, nothing in God's image, however imperfect and degraded, should be despised or neglected. And the developmentally disabled, more than all else, need human sympathies and protection. They are part of us, in our households, and we may not indulge the wish to ignore their presence or banish them from our minds."[87]

It wasn't until 1960 that it was concluded to recommend county systems to oversee programs for developmentally disabled persons funded by local, state, and federal funds. The JeffCo workshop is the successful Jefferson County program where both David and Ruthy used their talents. It also became the meeting ground for their budding romance.

David and Ruthy at a JeffCo Event[88]

86   Floyd, Barbara L. Editor. *From Institutions to Independence.* Published by the University of Toledo Press

87   Floyd, Barbara L. Editor. *From Institutions to Independence.* Published by the University of Toledo Press

88   Compliments of Ruthy Rodgers

Chapter 14

LET THE DATING BEGIN

As David got off the JeffCo workshop bus, he ran into the house to give his mom the good news!! This was in 1982, and David had been at the workshop since 1979. But David was in a different mood when he came home that day. In his usual style of excitement, he repeated, "Guess what! I have a girl friend – yes, yes, I have a girl friend!" As Dorothy smiled at his excitement, she said, "Well, that's nice. What's her name?" "Just a minute, just a minute," David said as he started to dump out his huge pockets. "I got it, I got it, darn somewhere." he said as his frustration grew through the sorting. Finally, a crumbled piece of paper was pulled from his pocket wreckage. Dorothy wasn't surprised that it took him so long to find a piece of paper in those huge pockets. Dorothy didn't say much about David's quirks, but Kathy had laughed when her mother, doing laundry one day said, "Can you imagine why he carries all these pens and tablets in his pockets and he can't even read or write?" Maybe it all was for this very day, when David proudly held out the piece of paper for Dorothy to read, "Ruthy Ellen Rodgers." Ruthy could write, so David had asked her to write her name so he could show his mother. That's how the Kelps family learned about their son's soon to be mate of 30 years!

David and Ruthy In Love[89]

As David prepared to go to the workshop the next morning, he announced that he was no longer going to be picked up at the corner, but rather he would walk the two miles to catch Ruthy's bus. And so every morning, rain or shine, he would be at the corner to meet Ruthy's bus and ride the few blocks to the workshop with her. It wasn't long until David concluded that he would also ride Ruthy's bus at the end of each day, all the way to Ruthy's apartment. They would follow their routine daily. When they arrived at Ruthy's they would walk to Value King on Market Street, buy the food for that night's dinner and food to pack their lunches for the next day. They would then fix dinner together with Ruthy's know how and David's strong hands to open the jars, and his height to reach up into the cupboards. After the dishes were done and the lunches packed, David would call Dorothy to pick him up at eight pm. It was easy to see immediately that this combination truly was a match! David provided Ruthy with security and strength. Ruthy could lend him her talents of reading and writing. But most of all, Ruthy got a happy family life that she had never known, and David found a *governor* for all of

89 Compliments of Ruthy Rodgers

his anger and misbehaving. With one look, Ruthy could get David to cease swearing, stop smoking, and stop drinking! David truly wanted to please Ruthy. When asking the calm David today, "Where did all that anger go?" He points to Ruthy and says, "She did it." The family remembers at a holiday buffet when David got upset because he was hungry and wanted to be first. Ruthy said one sentence, "If you don't behave yourself, I'll commit myself to Cambridge (state mental institution)." With that threat, David would *normal up* fast. No more angry David.

For this blessing of Ruthy, Dorothy would pick up David at 8 pm every night of her life from 1982 until 1997 – fifteen years, until she was 81 years old. Through rain, snow, ill health, etc., Dorothy would faithfully pick up her son. In the last few years of her life, as she laid in pain at Kathy's home, Kathy followed through to make sure David was home every night. Aunt Dorothy was a very moral person.

David and Ruthy were known as the King and Queen of the Jeffco workshop. They knew everything that was going on with everyone. The case workers said they were the rumor controllers. In asking Ms. Nolan if their relationship was unusual, she said, "She had never seen a relationship between two developmentally disabled individuals last this long." I'm sure one reason was the total inclusion of Ruthy with all family gatherings.

At The Game[90]

---

90 Compliments of Ruthy Rodgers

Their dating life was encouraged as Ed Kelps took them to a New Year's Eve party at Redman's CB farm. He even took them to drive-in theaters and would wait in the car, reading a book, if they wanted to go out to eat. When the dating began, Penny would allow Ruthy to bring David to their home before Ruthy moved out to be on her own. Penny also took Ruthy to the mall to meet David where the two of them would walk for hours and sit on the mall benches to *people watch*. In their time together, they would spend a lot of walking and *watching* moments.

David had no interest in moving out of his home. Ed had been very instrumental in purchasing a men's and women's home for the developmentally disabled when he was on the parent council of Jeffco. But as David would be asked if he would like to live there, he would always adamantly reject the idea with, "I'd get into trouble. Too much drugs in there. They'd steal my CB stuff." When Ed considered David's adult well-being, he probably never imagined that David would find a life partner with whom he would share his adult life.

The family readily took in Ruthy as a family member. Her name was Ruth Ellen Rodgers, but in their hearts she was Ruth Ellen Kelps! David and Ruthy were ready to go whenever someone would take them. On one excursion, Kathy remembers a stop at a Dairy Queen where David ordered a large size milkshake. As the clerk pointed to every cup size she had, David shook his head, "No." She was about to give up when all of a sudden inside the window popped David's full head into her small space. He proceeded to point out the large can on the top of her shelf that was probably a gallon of syrup or a topping container. The girl, in sheer fright, got down the gallon container and gave big Davey his big milk shake! I don't think he was ever forgotten at that Dairy Queen!

When Bev and Jim Lipinski took their seven children on their family vacations, they often included Davey and Ruthy. Jim is quite the outdoorsman and would take Davey fishing. Jim was very good to David. On one trip, the whole family plus David and Ruthy went to Holly River and stayed in cabins. David had met the camp ranger, who still asks Lip about Davey every time his family vacations at the cabins. He probably remembers David, aside from his size, because when David's cabin was getting low on firewood, David got on his CB and summoned the ranger to bring him more wood because he didn't want to be cold. Lip looked out the window to see the ranger delivering a truckload of wood to David's cabin – not a usual ranger service!

Whenever Ed would take David to a fishing camp, David would come back with buckets of blue gills. He would just walk around the docks and all the men would give him their catch of blue gills. Since David was adamant that he wanted to eat his treasure, Ed would have the tedious job of cleaning these small fish.

Fishing[91]

Ed would take both David and Ruthy on chartered bus trips to the Tennessee Jamboree to see Garth Brooks, Johnny Cash's home, Graceland, Niagara Falls, and of course, to all of his siblings' homes for visits and all holidays. Can you imagine, after all the years without family holidays, Ruthy was now celebrating with people who loved and cared for her!

---

91   Compliments of the Kelps Family

A Holiday With Family[92]

Every Sunday morning, Dorothy would drop David off at Ruthy's and proceed to her church to get there early enough to open the nursery. David and Ruthy would saunter down the street, hand-in-hand, to the Hardee's fast-food restaurant for breakfast together before they would walk over to the church for the service. They provided so much company for each other. Ruthy would say, "Davey was a good catch. I think he's handsome." They really did adore each other.

One year, Ruthy required surgery because she was walking on her toes. This surgery required 46 weeks of recovery and staying off her feet completely for 26 weeks. Of course, there would be no question, Ruthy would move in with Dorothy Kelps as her caregiver. There was no one else to take care of Ruthy!

The Kelps had helped Ruthy move into her first apartment. Then they moved her to the Rodger's Plaza, and then six years later to the Gaylord Apartments. There David and she share the memory of David sneezing, as they sat on her eighth floor balcony, and watched his false teeth go flying over the rail and onto the pavement. They laugh and giggle, even today, about that event.

92 Compliments of Ruthy Rodgers

Happy Ruthy and Toothless Davey[93]

She would live at the Gaylord's for fourteen years before Dorothy Kelps would pass away in 1999.

Everyone was afraid to tell David about the loss of his beloved *Mudder*. He had weathered the loss of his father, Ed Kelps, in 1986. His parents had gone out to eat at the Roadhouse Restaurant on Rt. 7 when Ed keeled over with a fatal heart attack. Dorothy though, was still around for Davey and Davey was still around for Dorothy for thirteen more years. But no one was sure how David would take the loss of his mother. With all the family pouring in from all different locations, it was concluded that brother-in-law, *Big Jim*, would be the one to deliver the bad news. As David was told about the death of his mother, he looked at Jim and said, "Well that's what happens when you get old." How peaceful Dorothy rested knowing that her son had the companionship of Ruthy.

---

93   Compliments of Ruthy Rodgers

At the conclusion of the funeral events for Dorothy, David announced to the family that Ruthy would now be moving into Dorothy's house to live with him. To which Kathy responded, "Oh no you're not! This house is too big and needs too much repair. Let's talk to Ruthy's case worker tomorrow." Even though David and Ruthy couldn't marry due to their government subsidies, Kathy probably could see the merit in both being under one roof to cut down on her evening *pickups*.

So the plans were put into motion to find government housing that David and Ruthy could share. They would pool their monthly paychecks and share expenses. Ruthy receives $600.00 per month from social security funds. David, however, gets $900.00 per month because Ed never claimed any funds for David until he retired himself. Periodically, before her death, Aunt Dorothy would give Davey extra money. Ruthy was their *tight* bookkeeper and check writer.

Their new living quarters were on the other hill in Steubenville. Kathy again moved Ruthy up to Pleasant Heights and moved David's belongings from Dorothy's house to David's new residence. In addition, Kathy had all of her parents' possessions from a three story home and fifty years of collecting to dispose of in the next few months.

As David and Ruthy settled into their new dwelling, on Sunday morning they would walk to a church a few blocks from their home. This is the church that Kathy's family attended. So every week, they faithfully would walk to their new church. After one service, David said to the preacher, "We want to join the church." The preacher didn't think much about the seriousness of David's request until the third Sunday when persistent David wanted an answer. The preacher set up a time and privately met with David and Ruthy to explain that even though they were welcome to worship with them, the church couldn't allow them to become members because they were living in sin. To this David objected and wanted more information. So the pastor continued to explain that since they weren't married, yet lived together, the church couldn't let them join as members. Of course, the reality was they couldn't be married, at least in the eyes of civil authorities. Even the pastor, realizing their determination, concluded to bring their situation to the board of the church. After some meetings, etc, it was determined if David and Ruthy would agree to a *commitment service*, they would be married in the eyes of God and could become church members. So a *wedding* was planned. Members of the church women's group asked if they could provide the reception for David and Ruthy after the *commitment service*. All the family and friends were informed, and David and Ruthy were so excited. Being committed to each other for life was exactly what they had expected since 1982 when they first fell in love. Of course, one aunt – my mom, was beside herself with distress over this obvious *sham*. "Well they are still not going to be married." she said. In fact, she wasn't even sure she could go and witness what she considered this *farce*.

As the day for the service came closer, she decided that she should attend as David's aunt. So the pews were full of all the Kelps family. The organ music started and the doors at the back of the church were opened. There stood David in his tuxedo and Ruthy in her white pantsuit with her corsage pinned on her shoulder. As she leaned onto David with her good arm, they slowly made it down the aisle. The preacher greeted them at the alter and said, "I have married a lot of couples that I thought had less of a chance of staying together than I believe of David and Ruthy's chances and commitment." To quote my mother, "There wasn't a dry eye in the place." Then she admitted, "I was sure wrong about that event!"

Ready To Be Married[94]

94 Compliments of David Kelps and Ruthy Rodgers

At The Alter[95]

The reception was lovely and Ruthy was delighted to cut the cake and open the presents and cards. As Ruthy opened the cards, David would comment, "$20.00, etc." When one card contained only $5.00, he said, "Only $5.00, that's ok."

_____

Let's Eat Cake[96]

Let the Party Begin[97]

So David and Ruthy remained David Kelps and Ruth Ellen Rodgers, but they could then become church members, as of January 22, 2000.

---

96   Compliments of David Kelps and Ruthy Rodgers
97   Compliments of David Kelps and Ruthy Rodgers

Chapter 15
MARRIED LIFE

As a *married* couple, I asked David and Ruthy once, "Do you two fight?" Both said "No." Then David said, "Sometimes we have disagreements." To which Ruthy replied with a little grin, "Yea but it is fun making up!" So all was well in their *marriage*!

It had been disappointing when their first choice of a house became unavailable. Right before they saw the house, a mill worker and his family were planning to buy the home, but David happily reports that it ended up that they finally did get that house when the other deal fell through due to mill layoffs. They both sympathetically talk about how bad the mill closings had been for the whole town. Ruthy said, "The city is sad. It's like the words of the song *Allentown* by Billy Joel, about the mill closings." In that song, he laments the closing of mills, unemployment lines, broken promises of success in life if they worked hard, and the pain of not having the future their fathers had through the past generations of work in the area.

Their home was a reflection of the down economy. In a once nice neighborhood, there now are drugs, rundown houses, and even shootings. With David's CB, he knew everything that was happening, good and bad, in Steubenville. When my friend who is a retired female police officer talked with David, she said, "He knows more about CB's and scanners than I knew existed." He's had fifteen CBs and currently has a 5980 magnum. He had to move his CB from his bedroom down to the first floor so that it didn't interfere with the neighbor's technology. Often David would be on his CB from 9 am to 9 pm, with Ruthy at his side.

David and Ruthy were good neighbors and had good neighbors. David would shovel the snow and cut grass for the neighbors. He had cut grass as a teen at Applecreek and at the workshop. When David ran out of milk, he would knock on the neighbor's door and they would drive him to the Maryland Market. Kathy would faithfully take them to the store once a month. They each had their baskets and could quickly navigate to get each of their desires for the month. David would get his four gallons of milk, but he would need to refill by the middle of the month. The excitement of the grocery store day was that they would eat at Wendy's next to the grocery store. That was their big day out each month.

Grocery Day[98]

So their *married* life began in their own little bungalow, and David and Ruthy started *to play house.* Their first summer, they decided to have a garden. They bought the seeds and planted them in their own backyard. However, the normal goal in a garden is not how large the produce can grow, but for David, *big is beautiful.*

---

98 Compliments of the author

David and His Prize Zucchini[99]

Their garden project only lasted one season. The produce was a little tough. Ruthy would say, "It didn't taste like things from my grandma's garden."

Their days often included their bus rides for errands and entertainment. They kept the city bus routes at their fingertips. David would hold Ruthy's arm and escort her over the curb and up onto the sidewalk for the block and a half walk to the bus stop. David would always open the door for Ruthy and let her go first. If someone was having trouble maneuvering the bus steps, David would jump to the rescue. David had been taught manners and how to treat a woman with respect by examples in his home. For their bus excursions, David would carry a large laundry bag to gather their purchases. In the winter, as he grew his beard for warmth, he would look a lot like a giant Santa Claus with his bag hung over his shoulder and Mrs. Claus on his arm.

99 Compliments of Ruthy Rodgers

But if there were purchases in the bag, they would be sure to tell you, "We save our money and if we don't have the cash then we don't buy." They also set up a rule that if either thought they wanted to buy something, they would wait until they had come back three times to the item and question, "Do we really need this? Do we really want to buy this?" Ruthy said most times, they would say, "No, we don't really need this." And of course when a bill came in the mail, it had to be paid that day. Kathy would get Davey's emergency call that, "No it can't wait until tomorrow!" Ruthy would say, "If you pay your bills right away they won't bug you." In all their years together, they only bounced one check. They had added instead of subtracted a transaction in their checkbook. Kathy kept a diligent eye and reminded Ruthy that David needed to sign his own checks. Kathy says David didn't understand that $4 + 4 = 8$, but he knew that $\$4 + \$4 = \$8$!

They also had rules about eating out. When their checks would come in the mail, the next morning they had to go to the bank. So they would rise early and walk the two miles out to the McDonalds right beside their bank. They loved McDonalds breakfasts and would talk to all the breakfast regulars at McDonalds. But never would they miss the opening of the bank. Prior to any employee's arrival, David and Ruthy would be at the door to greet the first bank employee and make their deposit. Then back home they would walk. On other days, they would take the bus downtown for lunch and greet the other patrons at PD's Restaurant (great food). Because I knew they liked eating there, I took them for lunch and asked if they ate there much. The answer, "Only if we have money. No money, we eat at home." We walked into their home one day to see a new flat screen TV. "Wow Davey, how did you get that?" I asked. Ruthy proudly responded, "The cable man said we needed a new TV, so we took all our change that we'd saved for one and a half years and Davey carried it to Walmart!" With the TV and stand, the total was $1,000.00 and they summoned a CB buddy with a truck to come to Walmart to pickup the items. They were savers!! Can you imagine the sight at the Walmart counter! Only a 7', 330# giant would dare carry that amount in change! They were very tickled and proud, and Ruthy giggled as they relayed the story of their purchase!

It was on a wintry day the first year they were married, that they summoned Dave's sister Kathy to their home. They couldn't wait to tell her what they had decided. "We want to take a vacation!" "Really?" Kathy responded. "Now where is it that you would like to go?" she asked. She was quite surprised when in unison they said, "Disney World! We have seen it on TV." "Davey that takes a lot of money." was the only response Kathy could give to this surprising request; even though many other objections immediately entered her mind – "like a seven foot giant, a crippled woman, and both developmentally disabled. How would this work for transportation, etc.?"

But David and Ruthy had the first objection covered much to Kathy's shock. "Wait, wait, wait here. I got to show you something!" David exclaimed bouncing up the steps to their bedroom. As he descended the steps with jars and a sack, Ruthy giggled, "We got money." To Kathy's gasp, David showed her a lot of money. "How much is there?" Kathy asked. Ruthy answered quickly, "We don't know, we can't count!" There was $8,000.00 they had saved together over time! "Wow, wow, wow, Davey we are going to the bank immediately!" Kathy exclaimed. The vacation was on the back burner of Kathy's thoughts! Getting robbed or shot was a more pressing concern!

So to the bank they went and then they immediately resumed the vacation conversation. As Kathy took them home, she said, "Let me call the family and see what we can do."

The day had come and David and Ruthy were beside themselves with giddy excitement as brother Ron had concluded that he would rent a van and get them a hotel room inside the Disney World grounds. Ron would take a course that week which was offered in Orlando, and David and Ruthy would *honeymoon* alone!

For an entire week David and Ruthy would do their favorite things, walk and watch people – no rides or shows except the monorail which would let them look and rest. They frequented every shop and in keeping with David's promise to spoil Ruthy, their only purchase would be a string of costume pearls and earrings for Ruthy. Their "Do we need it?" rule paid off compared to most of us who have lugged home lots of now lost or broken trinkets.

But there was one store that had a Mickey Mouse stick pin for a baseball cap. David really liked that pin! Everyday as they walked around the park, they would go into that store and David would gawk at the pin and try to barter a better price. But every day he would shake his head and leave the store mumbling, "Too much money, too much money!" It was on the last day, as they were eating ice cream cones and waiting for Ron to come get them that they saw the store owner coming towards them with a small box. As she placed it on the table she said, "Would you like the pin you have been looking at every day?" David said, "No, too much." She said, "It's free. I want to give you the pin as a gift." "Oh my, oh my!" Davey said ripping the box open and excitedly attaching it to his cap. Little did the young lady know that her kindness that brought such joy to a developmentally disabled man would be heralded for many to hear.

The vacation had been a success! Ruthy went home with pearls. Davey went home with his hat pin. And Ron *endured* the round trip ride to Orlando. Interestingly, when Ron reported the trip, he amazed us all that David's only eatery request was *Hooters* on the way home. Remember, the mind is disabled but not the hormones!! Ruthy giggles when Ron tells that story.

Back at home they settled into their normal routine. Most of the town knows David and Ruthy from their visible walks at stores, malls, and all the sidewalks of their community. They have probably walked every square inch of the city. How could anyone miss them? To quote Ruthy, "We are popular, everybody knows us. Like Mutt and Jeff!" she giggles. They know everything about the city – who owned what and what the building had been before, etc. It made for a very interesting ride around town with them on the public transportation. They knew every bus driver by name and loved to tell how they would give the drivers chocolate covered cherries for holiday presents. They also realized that as they would buy the bus driver a crab sandwich, a coke, and piece of pie often, as David loudly whispered to me, "Then they drop us right off at the door if its bad weather." They had realized *what goes around comes around*!

As David had promised to *spoil* Ruthy, he kept his promise. The lady at the jewelry counter at the mall was their friend. Sometimes they were looking and sometimes they were buying. At the time of their commitment service, Davey bought Ruthy a ring. Neither had noticed that as David had pushed the ring onto Ruthy's finger that it started turning black in a few days. When Kathy saw it, in alarm she said, "Ruthy does that hurt?" She admitted, "A little." Of course Kathy took her to have it cut off immediately. These times are the ones that remind us of their developmental disability conditions.

Ruthy sings along with the oldies songs playing in the store. When I complimented her that she knew the song, she smiled and said, "We may be old but we still remember." Then she continued through the medley never missing a word.

When asked if David and Ruthy still go to the same church, David says, "Won't let me – their system." Further, I learned that the issue is since David's legs had gotten older, he no longer could sit in the narrow pews – that was "their system" that wouldn't "let" him go to church. But Ruthy chimes in quickly, "We watch good TV preachers Sunday morning, like Schuller and Earnest Angley. We like them." she says.

David's legs made it hard to travel in a conventional car as he got older. It was always our pleasure to host the Reed family reunion at our home each summer. The last two years that we had the event, we sent a limo to David and Ruthy so that he could stretch his long legs. Now that was one happy camper, as David met the limo at his modest home. Of course, Davey and Ruthy would be ready. They were never late! Long before the pick up time, you could count on David and Ruthy sitting on the porch, ready to go. Davey was full of tales when he got out of the limo at our house. Truly they were King and Queen on those days! We knew where to find them all weekend. Davey, when not sitting with Ruthy, would be unsuccessfully fishing off the dock and Ruthy would sit on the porch in a rocking chair and look out over the water. We had so much fun at those family reunions. One year David's limo driver got lost on the trip and David had to guide her to our door. Directions were David's thing. Whether instructing a substitute bus driver, a new driver for Jeffco deliveries or a limo driver; that part of his brain worked overtime! Ruthy always took time when she got home to write me a thank you note. She is as sweet as they come.

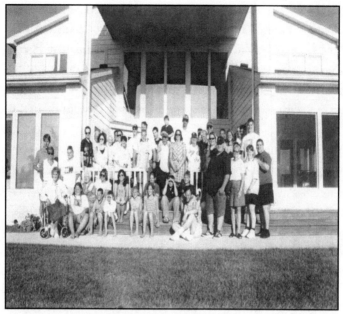

Family Reunion at the Michael's[100]

Enjoying the View[101]

---

100 Compliments of the Kelps Family
101 Compliments of the Kelps Family

Previous to Ruthy's involvement with the Kelps family, her caseworker says that she didn't make her own appointments or make her own decisions. However, she now is totally capable of doing those things and makes all of her own appointments. Her caseworker said Ruthy always had the ability to do more, but only now does she have the confidence to do what she does. She's even gotten to the point where she will take the bus by herself early in the morning if David sleeps later than usual. She says, "I go out to Walmart and walk around. I talk to people. There's lots of school teachers there and the clerks all know me. They say to me, where's your better half?" "Sometimes," she says, "I just ride the bus for a few hours and talk to the passengers and just look around the city."

On our historic trip to Cranberry, Pennsylvania to get David's favorite Krispy Kreme donuts, the subject of Ruthy previously being shy came up as we drove the hour to retrieve *the only donuts that will work* per David. It was cute to hear David chime in from his totally folded up posture in the backseat of my small car. "I tell her you can do it, Ruthy – you can do it, I tell her. Now she not shy!" David had learned the benefit of positive affirmations since he was a child persisting over and over again with his bike riding. His brother, Ron, would repeatedly say, "You can do it Davey," until Davey believed he could. He never quit. Now David has used this on Ruthy very successfully per her caseworker.

As David unfolded at the Cranberry, Pennsylvania Krispy Kreme store, he went around to help Ruthy get out of the car parked on a slanted parking lot. As we entered the store, no more excitement could be had than David seeing the glass wall showing the cascading famous glaze dripping onto hundreds of hot Krispy Kremes coming out of the donut maker! Hands started rubbing together, his mouth started salivating, and Davey with sheer joy in his voice loudly proclaimed, "Oh Boy, Oh Boy, Oh Boy – Ruthy look at those donuts! Oh Boy, Oh Boy!!" A gold mine couldn't have been more exciting than David's prospects of finally getting some Krispy Kremes! For some reason, all the sources for Krispy Kremes in Steubenville had dried up. We had all tried to satisfy David's donut cravings with every other great bakery brand donut. "No." he would shake his head. "It's not a Krispy Kreme." We bought six dozen that day of which the three of us polished off a dozen before we left the store! Ruthy would only have one and I had to talk her into that one. Four years earlier she been diagnosed with diabetes and not one bit of sugar had crossed her lips in four years. We took the remaining five dozen home, kept one dozen out and froze the rest. David would ration the balance daily.

David and Ruthy always had their *bags packed* and all of the family included them. Our dear Aunt would treat all of us cousins regularly to summer vacations in the Akron, Ohio area when we were children. Davey and Ruthy, as adults, would go visit our favorite aunt in the summer. They would take walks to the mall near her house. One day they recognized Earnest Angley's Church that Ruthy had watched on Sunday mornings. Ruthy couldn't believe her find. They also were taken to Sea World where David's retired uncle worked. When David fell and broke his glasses, our giving aunt got him a new pair. David and Ruthy were fun to give things to because they were extremely appreciative of even the smallest kindness shown to them.

They would go on CB Club bus trips and "Have a good ol' time!" per David. When they would come to our home, Eagle Isle, the family would always take David to nearby Cedar Point. He was always so funny because he would repeatedly say, "Too expensive, too expensive." He was always proud of our home near Lake Erie, and couldn't wait to show all of his neighbors pictures of our house. If David went anywhere, he would tell everyone. One time when on a vacation with his sister Bev's family, his brother-in-law Lip took him to find a Lego kit of a big truck. Now that was the highlight of that vacation for Davey. He worked tirelessly on the truck with the family's help.

Traveling one time with Kathy to see his brother Ken's family in Ravenswood, West Va., they stopped for lunch at a small restaurant. David was excited to have pumpkin pie. So after he ate, he ordered pumpkin pie with milk. Kathy stared as the waitress brought him a piece of pumpkin pie in a bowl of milk. David started eating it so Kathy didn't say anything until they got back into the car. Kathy turned to David and said, "Is that the way you wanted your pie?" David shook his head and said, "No, that was stupid!" But he never complained in the restaurant. Always lots of laughs with David. All of David's siblings have separate stories of how their children each, at junior high age, asked their parents, "Is Uncle Dave different?" David was so accepted and never derogatorily spoken of, that it took until seventh grade for four families of children to notice *something different with Uncle Dave.*

Beverly has a son who played college baseball for Youngstown University. I recently had some meetings with Jimmy's coach who is now a member of the FUS staff. He knew I was writing a book about a 'David'. But it didn't connect until one day I said David Kelps and he exclaimed, "Uncle Dave, Big Uncle Dave!" He had been taken to Jimmy's college ball games enough times that the coach knew "Uncle Dave!"

David's brother Ron lives in Nashville, so David and Ruthy visited his family and went to the Grand Ole Opry! He would tell you a lot about that fun trip and Ruthy would just grin and agree! She loved that music.

The Shrine Circus was in Wheeling, West Va., and so a family entourage of two of Beverly's children, one of Kathy's boys, and one of Ron's boys went, and of course they included Uncle Dave and Aunt Ruthy.

On one occasion, when David was visiting Ron and his wife Suzy, it was concluded that Suzy and Dorothy were going to go out to the store. So Ron and Davey would baby-sit Ron's small baby. When the phone rang and David had heard more crying than he wanted to hear, assuming it was Suzy on the phone, David yelled, "Tell her come home, baby crying!"

Of course with this close family, Ruthy and David were included in all the holiday festivities. On these days, Kathy never knew how she would find David dressed. One day, she told me, after one look at him with his new look of wearing baggy pocketed shorts over baggy pocketed jeans, "I have to pick my fights and this isn't going to be one today!" Wise sister. David was David!

It was always David's delight to hide the Easter eggs. Occasionally, he would have to be reminded that the eggs hidden eight feet in the air were a little high for his three foot nieces and nephews to find. As the siblings' children grew older and started to move away, the family would have holidays at a distance. David and Ruthy chose to celebrate by themselves to avoid the travel. They conquered a Thanksgiving dinner by themselves which they'll proudly tell you had all the trimmings and they enjoyed every bite!

David and Ruthy's traveling days together are over. In the last year, David's health has declined. He has been diagnosed with congestive heart failure and needs to sleep in a recliner. At the word *hospital*, there is a definite "NO." His legs have started to swell and his walking is a little slower. They would always say, "We get our exercise, we don't get tired, we just take it easy."

David at age 64 and Ruthy at age 66 retired from their Jeffco jobs in September, 2010. As the economy had changed and the community wasn't buying as much of their products, it had become boring with no work to do. They decided with David's health issues that it was time to retire.

They missed their friends, but David and Ruthy had figured out a long time ago how to enjoy each other. There's not much these two can't do together. Ruthy will say, "Davey's good company, he makes me laugh." Davey likes his two liter of Pepsi and bag of chips on the right side of his big rocker. Heaven forbid, don't move the chips to the left side. That messes up his routine. He sits every evening and looks through the entire Herald Star Newspaper even though he can't read! He even marks up the crossword puzzle!!? I asked Ruthy, "Do you check his puzzle?" She laughs and says, "No." Ruthy also does crossword puzzles and likes to do cross stitch. Ruthy looks over at Dave and tells me, "I think he's handsome." I asked them both, "What do you do for each other?" Davey first rips off his list:

"She:
- Keeps me in line
- Keeps track of my medicine
- Does errands for me when I'm sick
- Cooks
- Writes checks."

Ruthy then responded:

"He:
- Protects me
- Reaches things for me
- Buys me nice things
- Carries the laundry downstairs
- Helps me when I walk."

As we go out on their porch, they take their usual position on their glider and they start to rock back and forth.

Loving Life On Their Porch[102]

It's hard to imagine what these two have been through – the jeers, the laughs, the frustrations, and false institutionalization.

So I ask them, "Do you have any regrets?" They look up at me, stunned and say, "No, No, We Happy, We Happy!!"

---

102 Compliments of Jerry Hartley

Chapter 16

TILL DEATH DO US PART

It was a hot summer night at 10:30 pm when the Pavlik's phone rang. As the caller was identified as David's residence, Kathy said to Al, "This can't be good." She knew David and Ruthy were always asleep at this hour.

Ruthy told Kathy that David had fallen to the floor and could not get up. Ruthy, with her small five foot frame, had frantically tried to get David, all 330 lbs and 7 foot frame back up onto the chair. But she couldn't budge him.

As always, Kathy and Al responded immediately and rushed to help. It became obvious that even Kathy and Al did not have the strength to move David. Reluctantly, but understandingly, David finally agreed to calling the emergency squad.

With their bedroom on the second floor, the squad quickly evaluated that this was not going to be easy getting Davey down the steps and into the ambulance. As they asked David if he wanted them to take him to the hospital, he said, "No." The attendant looked at Kathy and said, "We can't take him unless he agrees!" Kathy quickly leaned over David and said, "Davey, don't you think it's time to get help at the hospital?" When David softly said, "I guess so." Kathy immediately turned to the attendant and snapped, "That's a yes!"

The next few minutes were rather hairy. Getting David's large frame down the steps and out the door looked almost impossible at points. But as they finally reached the porch, Ruthy would see David go through their door for the last time.

She followed to the hospital with Kathy and Al. Even though David had a living will, requesting no resuscitation, the decision required all of his siblings to be in agreement at the hospital due to David's developmental disabilities. So all of David's family flooded into Steubenville in the next twelve hours. David never said another word after, "I guess so." It was on August 5, 2011, that David would take his last breath.

They say a man's worth is in how much he is missed and how much he is thought of at his funeral. To see three rows of grown young adults, nieces and nephews, with tears flowing down their cheeks, was a blessed sight and honor to David Kelps. Ruthy stoically sat there and heard the tributes to the love of her life. The man who had given her security and a family was now gone. The preacher had spent the previous day at the Pavlik home with all the family, gathering details of David's life. The service included these words:

"Memories are a marvelous gift – you are remembering growing up with a special brother – a gentle giant who loved with his whole heart and never met a stranger – chocolate cakes that would be eaten as quick as Mom baked them, and a Dad who would give up trapshooting to pay for David's milk drinking – he simply worked his magic on others – he had a knack at bringing out the best in others – whether it was a fisherman, bus driver or truckers on a CB in Nova Scotia or you, his family – his approach was simple – be happy – love completely – don't worry about little things – if something is funny – laugh, even in church – don't concern yourself with what others think. David taught you to listen with your heart – and when he said Ruthy Blondie is mine – well you made quite the team – working together – and traveling – you were never left out – family vacations at the beach or fishing.

Well perhaps what is truly remarkable is the impact his life had upon all of you – he inspired us to see the world with a little more acceptance of others – to love completely without complete understanding.

The book of life is brief and once a page is read, all but love is dead – love is never lost – not even in death – it is hard in moments such as this to come to grips with the reality of such a loss – so we turn to faith, faith that allows us to remember and rejoice! Albeit with tears!!"

Goodbye David! So excited that you will be able to read this book from heaven.

Epilogue

Our Ruthy is doing fine, having changed to a new secured apartment with some of her workshop friends in residence. She gets Meals on Wheels, and Kathy and Penny are both in her life for other needs. She misses her David, but as always, for Ruthy life moves on with a smile.

Appendix

1. JeffCo Evaluations of David Allen Kelps and Ruth Ellen Rodgers.

2. Reference of Catholic/Protestant likes and dislikes from the book, "Let The Fire Fall", an ecumenical look at the work of Father Scanlan T.O.R.

Appendix 1

JEFFCO EVALUATIONS OF DAVEY AND RUTHY

This part of the book, hopefully, will serve several purposes:

1. To inform those who may question the issues of qualifying traits, abilities, supportive help, etc. necessary for independence to become a reality for the developmentally disabled.

2. To give all a respectful appreciation and overview through evaluations of two wonderful overcomers, Ruthy and David.

For the sake of those who may question more issues about the qualifications of David and Ruthy's ability to live independently, I have secured the permission from JeffCo Industries and both David and Ruthy to share with you their clinical evaluations.

The following words in quotes will be directly from the reports of the Jefferson County Board of DD (formerly MRDD).

Having not known the work of these agencies previously, I am very impressed with the atmosphere and the care shown to David and Ruthy. Information is gathered by caseworkers and professionals to secure issues of:

- Choices and options
- Personal income
- Housing
- Health
- Communications
- Appearance and hygiene
- Safety

- Unsupervised time at home, in the community, and transportation
- General well-being

Because of the above, as a taxpayer, the one ballet box I always mark with 'Yes' is for these developmental disability agencies to be funded for the continual and upgraded care of the developmentally disabled.

Neither Ruthy nor David considers themselves handicapped in any area. To quote Ruthy, "Everyone's handicapped in some area!" Their attitudes of overcoming, having happiness and peace are life lessons for us all.

Evaluations Quoted from Professionals:
David Kelps – 64 years old Ruth Ellen Rodgers – 66 years old

<u>Health Diagnosis:</u>

"David is diagnosed with mild retardation."

"David is an extremely large man. He has a history of hyperpituitary gland malfunction. He has peaked out with his disease at 7' tall. As a child and young adult, he was very intimidating to his peers and often was teased and taunted by his peers for amusement. He would often be baited into chasing other kids."

"David's intelligence quotient and his receptive hearing vocabulary suggest organicity."

"David displays some confusion in thought process."

"David communicates well. He is a close talker but will back off if you respectfully prompt him to do so."

"Ruth's medical diagnosis includes diabetes, physically handicapped left side due to hx spinal meningitis, mild mental retardation, glaucoma, left ear hearing impairment, high blood pressure, and hormone treatment."

"Ruth can administer all her medications."

<u>Assistance</u>

All the following are accepted duties assigned to David's sister, Kathy Kelps Pavlik. Kathy has been an angel of love for both David and Ruthy.

"Kathy is listed for Ruth Ellen's medical emergencies."

"Kathy is Ruth's representative in making major decisions."

"Kathy is Ruth Ellen's personal advocate and provides needed transportation."

"Kathy has Ruth's living will and is designated 'Attorney in Fact.'"

"Ruth has Kathy as Power of Attorney for medical issues."

"David relies on his sister, Kathy, for needed transportation" (and all of the above).

Kathy is not the legal guardian of either Ruthy or David, but instead, she has been a willing servant.

Workplace

"David was a very reliable worker."

"David is conscientious, requires no assistance, but will always seek help if he needs it. He is a steady worker and cleans his work area thoroughly."

"David's work performance is often above requirements. He corrects his own errors."

"Ruth has excellent communication skills. She is capable of expressing wants and needs verbally and written."

As Life Partners

"Ruth shares her home with her life companion, David. They lease their home from East Ohio Housing Corporation and access maintenance services through the Jefferson County Board of DD. Ruth and David manage to care for their home and know how to report their maintenance needs."

"Since David, Ruth has become very independent in handling her money, paying bills, shopping for groceries, personal needs, scheduling appointments, and riding the transit bus to access community services."

"Ruth has become increasingly independent in caring for her life needs. While she possessed skills to do most things for herself, Ruth lacked confidence in herself. She now was confidence and has made great strides."

"Ruth is independent with her appearance, hygiene and personal care."

"David is independent with appearance and personal care with verbal prompts when necessary from his partner, Ruth."

"David lives independently with his partner, Ruth, and he is at no risk to himself or to her."

"David is independent in the community with no risk to himself or others."

"Ruth is able to enter and exit vehicles independently, but exercises caution as she does so, since she has left side weakness from her meningitis diagnosis. Her significant other, David, offers assistance. David almost always accompanies Ruth."

"David is able to get wherever he wants to go."

"Ruth uses a cane as she moves about the community. But mostly she is escorted about the community by David, her housemate/significant other. He lends a hand if she needs support or assistance in climbing bus steps, etc."

"David makes his own choices. He relies on input from his life partner."

"Ruth is independent in cleaning their home, preparing meals and snacks, shopping for personal items and food and cleaning supplies. She is capable of writing a shopping list for her needs. Ruth can operate all appliances in her home and can independently operate her thermostat. There is a ramp attached to their home for easier access."

"Ruth is capable of determining the need for emergency services and knows how to call for assistance or help."

"David is able to contact and interact with his family."

"David is responsible for his own safety."

"Both Ruth and David express a desire to participate in the "supported living program" so that they could engage in social recreational activities. They are on the supported living waiting list at Jefferson County Board of DD. Ruth's SSA at JCBDD will assist in coordinating supported living services."

Retirement

"Ruth chose to retire in January, 2008, and is enjoying retirement."

"David worked at Jeffco Workshop since 1979. He retired in January, 2008. He now spends his time at home with his partner of 30 years, Ruth Rodgers."

"We talked about how things were going since she retired and she talked mostly about her companion and his new health issues. And that they did get a good report that his heart is stronger."

"In attendance besides David was his partner, Ruth Ellen, for the review. David continues to enjoy being retired. After doing a major house cleaning in the summer months with Ruth and his sister Kathy, their house continues to be kept at a good level of safety and cleanliness."

Appendix 2

THE ECUMENICAL CATHOLIC/PROTESTANT MOVEMENT AFTER VATICAN II

From, "Let the Fire Fall", by Father Mike Scanlon

My *extracurricular* activities were in many ways more important to me than the task of developing the college's academic program. Everything was happening at once in 1964. As the renewal of Vatican II was implemented, the winds of change started blowing like a gale though the Catholic church in the United States. I wanted to be part of everything that was new, and my position as dean gave me the perfect opportunity to do just that.

Ecumenical work came first. The Council's decree on ecumenism spoke very clearly about the common identity that binds all followers of Jesus Christ. It called on Catholics to "recognize the riches of Christ and virtuous works in the lives of others who are bearing witness to Christ, sometimes even to the shedding of their blood." To Catholics who might be reluctant or even afraid to enter meaningful relationships with Protestants, the Council said, "Whatever is truly Christian never conflicts with the genuine interests of the faith; indeed it can always result in a more ample realization of the very mystery of Christ and the church."

I tried to make this ecumenical vision a reality in the Ohio Valley. Ecumenical relationships in the area were about the same as they were everywhere else in the United States – that is, they were virtually nonexistent. Protestants and Catholics worked in the same offices, went to the same high school football games, and read the same newspapers, but they had almost nothing to do with each other as *Christians*. Many had difficulty acknowledging that the others were Christians at all. Cardinal

Mercier, the archbishop of Brussels earlier in this century and a great pioneer ecumenist, said that ecumenism begins with contact. "We have to encounter one another in order to know one another," he said. I set out to encounter all the Protestant leaders I could.

I joined ecumenical commissions and boards, preached in Protestant churches, gave retreats to Protestant groups, and encouraged other Catholic leaders in the Ohio Valley to do the same. In 1967, I preached at the service marking the 450th anniversary of Martin Luther's nailing the ninety-five theses on the door of Wittenberg Castle. I was the first priest ever to hold membership in the local YMCA (where I often played in volleyball games against other YMCAs). For three years, three other priests from the college and I spent two days a month with local Protestant leaders discussing our differences as well as our areas of agreement. We were the first Catholic priests many of these men of God had ever spoken to.

What did we talk about? We talked about the commitment to Jesus Christ we all shared, about our desire to serve him and his people, and about the practical and personal difficulties we all had as pastors of the church. We talked about our differences. Catholics and Protestants differ on many issues – the role of authority, the place of Mary, sacraments, principles for interpreting Scripture, styles of worship, and many others. The only basis for true ecumenism is a candid acknowledgment that profound differences do exist among Christians.

At the same time, these differences are not as great as many Christians think. Our discussions cleared up some misconceptions. Catholics do not worship Mary and the saints. Protestants *do* have appreciation for Christian tradition. Scripture *is* central in Catholic life. Protestants do not believe that "good works" have no value.

I came to see that many areas of Catholic life that the Protestant Reformation challenged were areas that needed change, or at least renewal. Catholics needed (and still need) a reaffirmation of the importance of preaching the word of God, of the centrality of God's inspired word in Scripture, of the need for personal appropriation of God's saving grace, of the doctrine of justification by faith, of the need for true repentance for sin and not just the sacramental action of absolution. Our discussions also helped Protestant leaders see the value of such "Catholic" ideas as the importance of unity, of authority in the church, the need of both Scripture and tradition, the universality of the church, and the importance of acknowledging and living out a heritage that traces back to the apostles.

Through my ecumenical work I came to realize that some of the most serious differences between Protestants and Catholics are cultural, not doctrinal and theological. They come from prejudices about "Catholic superstition" and "snake-handling holy rollers," ethnic hostility between poor Catholics of Slavic and Southern European descent and poor Protestants from the rural South competing for jobs in the steel mills. Much of the misunderstanding between Catholics and Protestants was exactly the kind of prejudice you would expect between communities that have little contact with each other.

I did my best to establish contact – that vital first step. Cardinal Mercier believed that contact leads to knowledge of one another, knowledge leads to love, and love leads to unity. I believe that we are on the road toward the fulfillment of that vision – the day when all Christians will experience the truth of Paul's words to the Corinthians, "Now you are the body of Christ and individually members of it" (1 Cor 12:27).

Years later, the College of Steubenville gave me an honorary degree for my ecumenical work.

Bibliography

Floyd, Barbara L. Editor. *From Institutions to Independence.* Published by the University of Toledo Press

Johnson, Alan, "Home No More: After 75 Years, Applecreek Center Closing Doors to Disabled Ohioans," *The Columbus Dispatch,* Columbus, Ohio

Scanlon, Father Michael T.O.R. *Let the Fire Fall.* Published by Servant Books, Ann Arbor, Michigan

Smith, Larry and Mason, Guy. *Images of America – Mingo Junction.* Published by Arcadia Publishing

Tosches, Nick. *Dino.* Published by Delta Biography

Homecoming Fiesta – Steubenville, Ohio. Published by Steubenville Homecoming Fiesta, Inc.

About the Author

MJ (Mary Jayne Reed) Michael is a business woman, owning several companies with her husband, Scott Michael, of 42 years. She was raised in Steubenville, Ohio until she left for Bowling Green State University in 1968. There she met her husband. They were married in 1970 and have resided in Fremont, Ohio, Scott's hometown, for most of their 42 years together.

They have two grown, happily married children and six grandchildren.

She writes this story from her heart with passion about her hometown of Steubenville, Ohio, and the inspiration from her Developmentally Disabled cousin, David, and his loving family.

This is MJ's first published book, with another book written by her family, 'The Building Blocks of a Functional Family', to be published soon.

She believes this book, 'The Gentle Giant and The Beauty Queen' will touch the hearts of all who read this true story.

- Mary Jayne Reed Michael is not a professional nor in any way related to any organizations for the developmentally disabled. MJ is the storyteller.

- Any dates or time frames mentioned in the story are Mary Jayne's remembrances of those items as told to her by many individuals.

- The story itself is a true story. All accounts mentioned have come from credible sources of family, friends, and professionals.

- It has been the goal of the author to relay all "pieces" of the tale, with close attention to its accuracy.

CPSIA information can be obtained at www.ICGtesting.com
Printed in the USA
LVOW062352150112

264006LV00002B/1/P